The
Power of
Preaching

The Power of Preaching

GARY WILKERSON

VODDIE T. BAUCHAM, JR.

CARTER CONLON

TIM DILENA

R. T. KENDALL

CLAUDE HOUDE

JOHN BAILEY

JOSHUA WEST

AMBASSADOR INTERNATIONAL
GREENVILLE, SOUTH CAROLINA & BELFAST, NORTHERN IRELAND

www.ambassador-international.com

The Power of Preaching

Gary Wilkerson, Voddie T. Baucham Jr., Carter Conlon, Tim Dilena, R. T. Kendall, Claude Houde, John Bailey, Joshua West

©2025 by World Challenge, Inc.

ISBN: 978-1-64960-761-4, hardcover
ISBN: 978-1-64960-635-8, paperback
eISBN: 978-1-64960-684-6

Cover Design by Efrain Garcia
Interior Typesetting by Dentelle Design
Edited by Katie Cruice Smith

Scripture taken from the The Holy Bible, English Standard Version. ESV® Text Edition: 2016. Copyright © 2001 by Crossway Bibles, a publishing ministry of Good News Publishers.

Ambassador International titles may be purchased in bulk for education, business, fundraising, or sales promotional use. For information, please email sales@emeraldhouse.com.

AMBASSADOR INTERNATIONAL
Emerald House
411 University Ridge, Suite B14
Greenville, SC 29601
United States
www.ambassador-international.com

AMBASSADOR BOOKS
The Mount
2 Woodstock Link
Belfast, BT6 8DD
Northern Ireland, United Kingdom
www.ambassadormedia.co.uk

The colophon is a trademark of Ambassador, a Christian publishing company.

Table of Contents

Chapter 1
The Power of Preaching: An Introduction

Gary Wilkerson

As church leaders, our job is to bring glory to God and transform people's lives. But we can only accomplish that if we have a correct, weighty view of God. Our souls need to be immersed in the presence and holiness of God.

This book is a collection of sermons *by* preachers *for* preachers. Originally presented online as a pastors' conference, these messages are a call for the power of the Holy Spirit to break through our low view of God through the crisis of our times. Our prayer is that these messages would stir your heart to prepare with passion, to pray with passion, and to preach with passion. Our desire is that these messages will increase your passion for preaching in such a way that on a Sunday afternoon, a topic for the next weeks and months will already be stirring in your heart.

We also hope these messages will bring some conviction to the necessity of returning to a place where we all preach with the power of the Holy Spirit—not in our fleshly energies nor from our desires, our ambition for success, nor from striving for fame. May that passion lead to prayer, spiritual and emotional preparation, and digging into the Word—not just reading the

Scriptures for sermons. May it lead to you having a deep hunger for the Word of God. May you be changed; may your ministry be changed; and may the people who listen to you be changed. And may God be glorified.

We desire that, at the end of this book, we would all come humbly before God and say, "God, this is Your Word. We are here to preach it with the power you would give to us, not in our own strength."

✚

Without knowing God—His majesty and holiness, love, graciousness, tenderness, long-suffering, wrath, justice, and judgment—it is impossible to preach with power. Without knowing God in His fullness, the power of our teaching will be limited to the limited knowledge we have.

Daniel 11:32 says, "The people who know their God shall stand firm and take action." I pray that as a preaching man or woman of God, you would come to the pulpit week after week being strong, your soul immersed in the presence and passion and holiness of God, and that you will preach with great exploits, seeing many lives transformed.

In our culture, there seems to be a disappearance of the greatness of God's glory. Even more disturbing is that even in our churches, there is a low view of God. We see God as less than He is—less grand, less glorious, less high and lifted up, less exalted even as "the train of his robe filled the temple" (Isa. 6:1). And when the church has a low view of God, what hope is there for our culture to have anything near a high view of God?

There is a great need for us as clergy to be reminded of God's greatness. And there is a great need for us to remind our people of the weightiness of God as we preach to awaken and restore in them a fresh view of the holiness, the majesty, and the splendor of God. If you have a low view of God, your preaching will reflect that. And if you have a high view of God, your words, your passion, and your soul will likewise reflect a high view of God—His holiness, majesty, splendor, wonder, otherness, and transcendence.

Many years ago, my father had the privilege of speaking at R. T. Kendall's church. A pastor introduced him, saying, "Here is David Wilkerson. Here is a man who has the weightiness of God when he speaks."

This pastor was referring to the Hebrew word *kavod,* which means "glory." This is not about glorying in ourselves. It has nothing to do with glorying in our eloquence. This kind of glory invites the weightiness of the glory of God. This weightiness does not carry a heaviness in the sense of it being a morbid, depressing, angry, or frustrating word. It is a word that uplifts. And the thickness of the cloud of the presence of God surrounds the people of God as they listen.

So our desire with this book is for pastors to move away from having a low view of God—as a God Who exists for our whims and wants and those of our congregations. We desire to see us all move away from the shallowness of our time and embrace a view of the depths of God, Who is more awe-inspiring and more amazing than we have ever thought or imagined. The littleness of our theology, our doctrine, and our view of God bring littleness to our lives. We end up not having the grand and glorious, amazing, wonderful, abundant life Jesus promised we could have.[1] "The church has surrendered her once lofty concept of God and substituted it for one so low, so ignoble as to be utterly unworthy of thinking, worshipping men," A. W. Tozer said.[2]

We try our best to bring God down to our size. We piddle around in little puddles rather than striving through the crashing waves in the fearsome depths of knowing Who God really is. That is having a low view of God. We have put God in the friend zone, rather than offering Him the depth of our love, not seeing Him as the One with Whom we would spend eternity. We have moved from an awestruck, trembling, crying out in near-death fear of the Lord to a "woe is me, I can hardly move" experience of the presence of

---

1   See John 10:10
2   A. W. Tozer, *On the Almighty God: A 366-Day Devotional* (Chicago: Moody Publishers, 2020).

God and then to a view of a God Who seems to be in our debt, required to meet our demands.

And if God doesn't meet our demands, He will experience our wrath. He will experience our rejection. He had better not displease us; He had better not require too much from us. He had better be kind in His support of us. He had better be a type of support system for our lives. We have turned God into our assistant, a genie, or a butler to get things for us, a need-meeter, a personal-fulfillment guide, a fortune provider, a well-being guru, a health insurer, our fame agent, our entertainment system.

We have made God into the kind of god to whom we might say, "I will draw close, read my Bible, pray, and go to church so I can get the life I want—a life free of pain, one where you will assure I'll meet my life goals. The benefits of the heavenlies will be all mine because I put in the time and the energy." How ludicrous! God never agreed to play the role of such a utilitarian god.

The Church in our generation has an overfamiliarity with God while at the very same time barely knowing Who He is. We have a casual attitude when we come into his presence. We are more familiar with him as Daddy, Friend, Partner, Helper. God is, indeed, those things; but we're more familiar with that part of Him while being oblivious to the majesty, splendor, transcendence, and otherness of God—those attributes of God that seem to be missing from our pulpits today to a great extent.

God is bigger; He is greater, more glorious, more powerful, more wonderful. And if we don't preach that power, that splendor, that wonder, that majesty of God, we are preaching a small message. The small God we proclaim will produce small lives. We will make small disciples who have small hearts, small passions, small prayer lives, a small hunger for the Word of God, a small interest in evangelizing the lost, and a small interest in missions.

When we approach God as small, God says to us, "You think I am just like you. You think I'm down on your level, that you and I are equal. You think I get a little bit of what I want, and you get a little bit of what you want; and we just sort of work things out together. No! I am God. I am high, and you are low."

We will never have a high view of God when we have a high view of ourselves—even if we put ourselves on an equal level with God. When God says in Exodus 20:3, "'You shall have no other gods before me,'" He is not only talking about not having an idol but also bringing something of ourselves, of our flesh, of our own will into His presence. In doing so, we are breaking one of the great commandments of God.

A low view of God belittles our preaching and diminishes the power in the pulpit. It leads to us filling our worship hour with pep talks, pop psychology, and motivational speeches with a slight sprinkling—a slight mention—of God. We might add a little prayer at the beginning or the end and call it good. Or we might read a passage from the Scripture but end with a message far from the message of the Scripture itself. In doing so, we are swimming in a kiddie pool, while the depths of the ocean call out to us. We nibble on snack packs with no nutritional value, while eight-course feasts are available to us in the presence of God. We nonchalantly climb a three-step ladder when we are called to the heights of a throne room far above anything we've ever dreamed or imagined. We squeak our toy trumpets when a symphony of the greatness and the glory of God is available to be resounded in churches across the nations. As a result, we as preachers leave people malnourished and facing a famine for the Word of God.

How do we dare gather in God's name if the focus of our gathering is not on God? Why preach self-help when we desperately need God's presence and power delivered to our people? Why settle for so little? Why divert God's people from their higher calling? Why leave them weak to the hardships of life? Why leave them unaware of the greatness and glory and majesty of God?

We live in perilous times. We have seen more trouble come about than we have seen in the last few decades put together. And a low view of God leaves us unable to address the dilemmas and crises of our time. But when we preachers raise our view of God, it moves our souls *and* the souls of our flocks to pursue God. It stirs up a longing to know God, to capture a glimpse of that which is much higher and greater than any of us. This is humbling.

As we humble ourselves before God, He lifts us up.[3] But this is not about getting a larger platform, a larger church, more fame, or more fortune. It is an exaltation of knowing the splendor, the majesty, and the glory of God. This is what Jeremiah speaks of when he says, "'Don't let the wise boast in their wisdom, or the powerful boast in their power, or the rich boast in their riches. But those who wish to boast should boast in this alone, that they truly know me and understand that I am the LORD who demonstrates unfailing love, and who brings justice and righteousness to the earth, and that I delight in these things'" (Jer. 9:23-24).

That is what we glory in. And that is how God glorifies us. God exalts us by saying, "Come to know Me. And in knowing Me, in coming out of your low view of Me and into My presence, you will see My power raised up in your ministry like never before."

In our churches, we hold God lightly. And when the church has a low view of God, what of the world? As goes the Church, so goes the culture. God is far above all, yet our culture drags His name through the mud. It outlaws God in our schools and ignores Him in the marketplace. Our culture banishes God from Hollywood, shuns God in Washington, scoffs Him on Wall Street, and despises Him in the laboratories of scientists who say they have no other god but their knowledge.

Humanity has a low view of God because the Church has a low view of God. We want to be like the world rather than becoming like God, like Christ. We want acceptance. We want our churches to be approved by men and women. We want fame and notoriety. We want to make God more palpable,

---

3   1 Peter 5:6

more accessible, and easier to grasp. We want to water down God. We want to contain Him. And in doing so, we've made God's Word easier to hear and easier to swallow.

A small God fits better into our pews and in our pulpits. If He's a God Who helps us in everything we seem to want or need, Who accomplishes for us that which we strive for, then He is our God. We want to make God in our image. Theology and doctrine are missing from our pulpits. Our doctrine has become more about us. Our singing is more about us.

Today, people walk into church hoping for a message that would help them be more successful and feel good about themselves. But that is a failure of a Sunday service. We ought to walk out of church saying, "I met God today. I sensed His presence. I was restored. I was touched by the presence of God."

This low view of God needs to be reversed, which is what we hope this book will do. We pray these messages will stir up a hunger and a thirst for God, that it will get inside your soul, gut, and spirit and put a spiritual hunger in you—a frustration, if you will—to say, "I can't carry on. If I don't come to the pulpit with a word from God, I won't get into the pulpit."

God, in His mercy, is willing to call us back to know Him, to hold a high view of Him. He is willing to call us back to the high things of God, calling us back to His presence once again.

✝

In his bestseller, *Knowing God*, first published in 1973, J. I. Packer suggests that many are leaving the church because churches have allowed God to become remote.[4] We sing songs and hear self-help talks, but they do not penetrate our hearts. This has led to a famine for the Word of God, a famine of the knowledge of God, knowing that God is self-revealing and

---

4   J. I. Packer, *Knowing God*, 8th ed. (Lisle: Intervarsity Press, 2021).

yet lacking hunger for the knowledge He wants to reveal to us. There exists a spiritual famine—not because God doesn't *want* to bring forth His Word from every pulpit in every part of this world but because the Church is not eating of it.

Jeremiah the prophet says, "Your words were found, and I ate them, and your words became to me a joy and the delight of my heart," (Jer. 15:16). Jeremiah was searching. He was studying. He was hungry. And once he found God's words, he digested them.

What you eat becomes a part of who you are. When you eat junk food, you destroy your body. Eat healthy food, and you become healthy. When you devour the Word of God, you become fervent, alive, holy, reverent. You become different. And you become somebody who has something to offer our famished culture.

Though you may hold a low view of God, God does not cease to be pure, holy, perfect, majestic, wonderful, nor all-surpassing. God does not cease to be loving, kind, gracious, wise, nor unchanging. Nor does he cease to be all-knowing, all-seeing, nor omnipotent. Your view of God doesn't change Who God is. He doesn't need you to make Him higher. He cannot be any higher than He is. All you need to do is to come to know Who He is. Then you begin to describe and proclaim what you have seen and heard, what you have come to know of God from God. He is not just loving; He is infinitely loving. God is not just holy; He is infinitely holy.

God is *for* God. God is *about* God. It's not that God doesn't care about us, our needs, and our desires. It's not that God doesn't love us. But God's love, in its greatest form, demonstrates Who He is and makes Him known.

God knows how to care for you. He knows how to love you. He knows how to touch you. But He also knows that your best life is not about how much you can acquire. It's not about what you can achieve. It's not about riches, honor, nor fame.

Your best life is one centered on knowing God. God rules and reigns in majesty over all men, women, angels, demons, circumstances, nations, kings, powers, rules, and authority. This is the God you and I can know.

Remember what Jeremiah says: "Let not the wise man boast in his wisdom, let not the mighty man boast in his might, let not the rich man boast in his riches, but let him who boasts boast in this, that he understands and knows me, that I am the Lord'" (Jer. 9:23-24).

If you have a high view of God, you will come to the pulpit able to speak about God like very few in our modern age. You will have something of God that is different. You will preach sermons that are a holy word from God that shakes you to the core.

✚

There are two ways you get to a low view of God. One is to have once held a high view, which has since diminished. The other is to have never held a high view of God. How can you restore or gain a high view of God? It takes a willingness to go against the tide of culture and the popular church trends, to seem unimportant, to have a vision of God, and to have a big God and a small self rather than a big self and a small God. Then alone can you experience what Isaiah describes: "I saw the Lord sitting upon a throne, high and lifted up; and the train of his robe filled the temple" (Isa. 6:1).

You don't approach preaching with a view of *you* being high and lifted up. It is not about your people leaving after you have preached, saying, "What a great preacher! What a great word they brought today." Instead, they will say, "What a great God we serve. What a high, holy, majestic, and lifted-up God we serve."

But you cannot accomplish this in your own strength. So we pray that as you read these chapters, God would fill you with power from on high so you would not just be learning some new tidbits or tips or gain some insights so you can preach a little bit better and feel good about yourself.

✚

In chapter order, this book includes messages by these pastors:

Voddie T. Baucham, Jr. serves as the dean of theology at the African Christian University in Lusaka, Zambia, where he also pastors a local church. Voddie shares about preaching pastorally as well as on presentation.

Gary Wilkerson is the president of World Challenge. I share about preaching with the presence of God.

Carter Conlon was the senior pastor at Times Square Church in New York City for many years. His heart is not just to preach good, interesting, or inspiring sermons but also to preach powerful sermons that change lives. You can look forward to reading what he has to share about preaching *for* people.

Tim Dilena—currently the senior pastor at Times Square Church—has close to forty years of pastoral leadership experience. He shares about the preparation and the prayer that goes into preaching.

Claude Houde is the pastor of one of the largest French-speaking churches in the world based in Montreal, Canada. Claude also has a Bible school that teaches French-speaking pastors to go throughout the world. His chapter is on preaching with passion.

R. T. Kendall pastored Westminster Chapel in London for twenty-five years. He knows how to preach in ways that transform people's lives; hence, his chapter is on preaching with power.

John Bailey is currently the vice president of ministry and operations at World Challenge, as well as a preaching voice for the ministry. His chapter is on preaching biblical repentance.

Joshua West is an author and preaching voice for World Challenge, as well as the executive director of the World Challenge pastors network, and his chapter is on preaching as proclamation and for the glory of Christ.

As you read their messages, may you see God. May God strike you with a sense of Who He is—His might, splendor, and majesty. May He keep you from smallness of thought, heart, mind, study, passion, and the view of God. May God once again give you a high and lifted-up view of Who He is and may that change everything about your preaching.

Chapter 2
Preaching Pastorally

Voddie T. Baucham, Jr.

Do you believe all Scripture is "breathed out by God and profitable for teaching"[1]? If you want your congregation to grow, you must present a balanced view of Scripture. You must address pressing needs and cultural moments and do it with a commitment to the core of gospel preaching.

I would like to look at the topic of preaching pastorally from a theological and philosophical perspective and then look at some practical applications. To do that, let's look at a passage in 2 Timothy 3 to see what this text says about the Bible and extrapolate what the text says to us about preaching the Word of God.

The apostle Paul told Timothy, "All Scripture is breathed out by God and profitable for teaching, for reproof, for correction, and for training in righteousness, that the man of God may be complete, equipped for every good work" (2 Tim. 3:16-17). The passage does not say *some* Scripture is breathed out by God. No, *all Scripture* is breathed out by God. And all Scripture is not only *suitable* for preaching but *must* be preached in order for the body of Christ to be equipped for every good work.

---

1   2 Timothy 3:16

As pastors, though, we tend to preach sermons not from the entire canon of Scripture but from only a fraction of the Word of God. When we do that, we are not giving our people a balanced diet; and without a balanced diet, they cannot grow. Nutritionally speaking, serving your family a well-balanced diet is about making sure you're serving a balance of macronutrients—carbs, fats, and proteins—along with micronutrients—vitamins and minerals. Imagine if you were to feed your children an all-carb diet, and in such an all-carb diet, you fed them mostly starch. If that's what you're doing, your children won't be very healthy at all.

This is what is happening to a lot of people in terms of the preaching they're receiving. We tend to preach almost exclusively from the New Testament. And from the New Testament, we tend to preach almost exclusively from the epistles, especially the Pauline epistles. So we are guilty of serving up an unbalanced diet of mostly the letters of Paul—the nutritional equivalent of feeding our people an all-starch diet.

Granted, it's easy to gravitate toward Paul because of the way he writes. He makes a point, and then he breaks down his point further. This makes it easy to find sermon points when preaching Paul. (I recognize the irony that this message is based on a passage from one of Paul's letters.)

Familiarity is one reason that we turn to Paul. But it's not just familiarity with the New Testament and Paul's epistles but also a lack of familiarity with the Old Testament. We don't tend to spend a lot of time in the Old Testament. I believe it's because we don't know how to interpret the Old Testament. Our hermeneutic does not equip us to see and discern—let alone preach—the gospel of the Lord Jesus Christ from *all* the Scripture. We don't see the gospel when we look at Old Testament passages. And because we don't see it, we don't preach it.

For those of us who tend to work in Scripture in the original languages, we tend to be a lot more familiar with Greek than we are with Hebrew. When we're doing an exegesis, we can dig into the Greek New Testament a lot better than we can into the Hebrew Old Testament. This is a linguistical problem. So hermeneutics and linguistics have become barriers to understanding and preaching from the Old Testament.

A Balanced View of Scripture

There was a study done among church members and pastors. Members were asked, "What book would you most like for your pastor to preach a series from?" The answer was Revelation.

Meanwhile, pastors were asked, "What book would you least like to preach a series from?" The answer? Revelation.

People want to hear sermons from Revelation because they don't understand it. Preachers *don't* want to preach sermons from Revelation because they don't understand it. I believe it's because Revelation quotes the Old Testament more than any other book in the New Testament. And if we don't understand the Old Testament, we cannot understand Revelation. What we understand the least about the Old Testament are the prophetic literature and apocalyptic literature. Revelation quotes all but two books in the Old Testament with most of the references coming from Isaiah and Daniel—prophetic literature and apocalyptic literature!

The same is true for the teachings of Jesus. Jesus preached from the Old Testament. This means that our lack of familiarity with the Old Testament is hugely problematic. If we do not preach from the Old Testament, we're robbing our people of this rich heritage; and we're not helping them be able to understand Jesus' teachings. The same is also true of Paul. We do not fully understand Paul's messages because he was trained in the Old Testament. And when he says, "All Scripture is breathed out by God," Paul is speaking about the Old Testament. Those were the Scriptures being taught at the time. The New Testament was still being written.

But the Bible as we have it today—Genesis to Revelation—was given to us by God, and God intends for us to preach all of it. When we do not preach both the Old and the New Testaments in their entirety, we're neglecting our people by feeding them an unbalanced diet, one that inhibits their growth. For your congregation to grow, you must present a balanced view of Scripture. You must preach from all of the Old Testament and all of the New Testament. Do not cherry-pick the Bible.

Some preachers—even hardcore expositors—will say they'll concentrate and preach through the New Testament. I was at my friend's church when they celebrated the fact that this friend, John MacArthur, had finally preached through every verse in the New Testament. Not long after, he told a group at a conference, "Somebody asked me if I'm now going to preach through the entire Old Testament. Look at me," he said, pointing at his white hair. "There's no way I'd make it through it all." But what he did was to preach on some Christological passages in the Old Testament, not verse by verse through an entire book. This friend is an expositor, and he'll eventually get into more of it.

But for many of us, we would only go to famous passages in the Old Testament, where it's easy to point to the person and work of Christ on the cross. Then when we are asked to preach the Old Testament narrative, right through the book of Isaiah verse by verse, we are not so inclined. And we would not even chance preaching through Exodus verse by verse, let alone Numbers!

If what Paul is saying here is true, though—and we know it is—then it means we cannot just preach on Isaiah 53 and say, "Jesus is the suffering Servant." He absolutely is. But what about every other chapter and verse in Isaiah? And what about every chapter of every book in the Old Testament? We would agree that all of the Bible is God's Word. Judging by what we tend to preach on most, does it show that we believe the Old Testament? Still, even if we never preached from the Old Testament or rarely preached anything but the Pauline epistles, we may believe there are *some* verses, *some* stories, and *some* passages hidden in the Hebrew Scriptures that are breathed out by God and need to be treated as such. We wouldn't dare say the rest of the Bible is *not* from God. But many would say—at least through our actions—that *perhaps not all* of the Bible is as "profitable for teaching, for reproof, for correction, and for training in righteousness." That's not what Paul says, though. Paul says all of it is profitable. And if you cannot see, translate, and communicate *how* profitable all Scripture is, that is *your* problem, not the Bible's.

There is no area in a believer's life where the Bible is irrelevant.

"What about science?" you may object. "The Bible isn't going to give us the mathematical calculations of the universe." That is true. The Bible isn't a scientific textbook, but the Bible teaches us how we ought to think about this universe God created and how to think about science rightly.

"What about culture?" There is also no issue in our culture where the Bible somehow has to take a back seat—not a single one. Paul says in verse seventeen, "That the man of God may be complete, equipped for every good work." That is why we need to preach the whole counsel of God because it is what God uses to prepare and equip His people for every task to which they are called. To be prepared for the work to which God had called us, we all need a well-balanced diet. And as pastors, from a theological and philosophical perspective, we must be committed to serving up such a balanced diet.

Practically speaking, how do we do this? We begin by addressing our hermeneutic.

A Gospel-Centered Hermeneutic

In Luke 24:13-15, we read, "That very day, two of [Jesus' disciples] were going to a village named Emmaus, about seven miles from Jerusalem, and they were talking with each other about all these things that had happened [Jesus having been crucified and His body being gone from the tomb]. While they were talking and discussing together, Jesus himself drew near and went with them." There they were, walking along the road to Emmaus; and Jesus joins them on their journey.

The fact that another person joined them on their walk wouldn't have been something uncommon. After all, there were other travelers walking in the same direction. There were also bandits along the way; it wouldn't have been strange for someone who was walking alone to have joined up with others. There was safety in numbers.

Luke continues in verses sixteen through twenty-seven:

> But their eyes were kept from recognizing [Jesus]. And he said to them, "What is this conversation that you are holding with each other as you walk?" And they stood still, looking sad. Then one of them, named Cleopas, answered him, "Are you the only visitor to Jerusalem who does not know the things that have happened there in these days?" And [Jesus] said to them, "What things?" And they said to him, "Concerning Jesus of Nazareth, a man who was a prophet mighty in deed and word before God and all the people, and how our chief priests and rulers delivered him up to be condemned to death and crucified him. But we had hoped that he was the one to redeem Israel. Yes, and besides all this, it is now the third day since these things happened. Moreover, some women of our company amazed us. They were at the tomb early in the morning, and when they did not find his body, they came back saying that they had even seen a vision of angels who said that he was alive. Some of those who were with us went to the tomb and found it just as the women had said, but him they did not see." And [Jesus] said to them, "O foolish ones, and slow of heart to believe all that the prophets have spoken! Was it not necessary that the Christ should suffer these things and enter into his glory?" And beginning with Moses and all the prophets, [Jesus] interpreted to them in all the Scriptures the things concerning himself.

I hope you didn't miss Jesus calling these disciples "foolish . . . and slow of heart"—not because they didn't believe all that Jesus Himself had foretold them but for not believing all that the prophets had spoken. In other words, Jesus preached Jesus from the Old Testament. So should we. But we have a hermeneutical problem. We think the only way we can go to the Old Testament and preach Christ is if we find one of these prophetic passages and can go to the prophecy that was fulfilled. That is not what I'm talking about here, nor am I talking about allegorizing the Old Testament when you look at every story in the Old Testament saying, "This has to mean this . . ." What I mean is that we must have a hermeneutic that understands that the Bible is a unit—a single unit that tells a single story. This is referred to as a *gospel-centered hermeneutic.*

Having a gospel-centered hermeneutic when we read the Bible, we're reading it as a unit. We read it as a historical narrative about God's redemptive work with His people and His faithfulness to His people that would culminate in the coming of the Person and work of Christ. When we look at the law of God, we're looking at things in the ceremonial law that point forward to what Christ will do when He comes as the ultimate Sacrifice.

When we see the civil laws and the moral laws, we're seeing the laws that condemn us because of our inability to keep them. But we're also seeing the laws that point to Christ and affirm Him as the One Who keeps the whole law on our behalf. When we're in the Old Testament, whether we're looking at the law or a narrative or whether we're looking at prophetic literature, it all points toward Christ. It is all ultimately about Christ.

We need to have a hermeneutical commitment, a pre-understanding that when we are in the Old Testament, we are looking at what God has done to pave the way for Christ. I do not have time here to go into everything we need to know and understand regarding the gospel-centered hermeneutic. But I commend you to be committed to understanding what it means to look at all of the Bible as a unit pointing toward Christ. And I urge you to preach the Bible from this perspective. That's the first practical thing we all must do. We must commit to growing in the way we understand the Bible.

In *Joseph and the Gospel of Many Colors,* I teach Christ from Genesis 37-50. I demonstrate how this narrative points us to the person and work of Christ.

I recommend that you do this as well. I urge you to read works by others who have done tremendous work in this regard.[2] If we don't understand how the Old Testament is connected to the New Testament as a single story, then we're not likely to preach from the Old Testament. And when we do that, we're not feeding our people a balanced diet.

Practically speaking, one way our congregation committed to serving up a balanced diet was to read and preach through the entire Bible. Part of our regular Sunday liturgy is to read a chapter from the Old Testament and a chapter from the New Testament—unless it was a ridiculously long chapter, in which case we broke it up. But we read the entire chapter. This means there's a significant amount of reading during the service both from the Old Testament and from the New Testament. We'll sing a song, read a chapter from the Old Testament, sing another song, and read a chapter from the New Testament. We do not read books in order, though. We go back and forth in terms of genres. After reading through Genesis, for example, which is part of the books of the law, we'll switch to a historical narrative, say, reading the book of Joshua. And after we finish Joshua, we'll read through one of the prophetic books, then wisdom literature, poetry, and apocalyptic literature. That way, we cycle through all the genres and all the books in the Old Testament.

We do the same with our New Testament reading. We'll read through one of the Gospels; then we'll read one of Paul's letters, then one of the general epistles, like Hebrews. And we'll read Revelation (apocalyptic literature) and the Acts of the Apostles. This way, our congregation reads through all the genres and books in the Old and New Testaments. This is a very important piece of this puzzle because the Bible tells us to give attention to the public reading of the Word.[3] But we do not end with reading. We also preach through all the books.

---

2   Start with books by Ed Clowney, Graeme Goldsworthy, and Bryan Chappell.
3   Biblical examples of the public reading of Scriptures are found in Exodus 24:7; Deuteronomy 31:9-13; Joshua 8:34-35; Nehemiah 8:1-12; Luke 4:16-21; 1 Thessalonians 5:27; Colossians 4:16; and Revelation 1:3.

We don't necessarily do it in one shot, especially with some of the bigger books—Genesis, for example. I believe we did a verse-by-verse exposition of Genesis 1-6. And then we took a break and went to Matthew, and we did the first few chapters there. And then we went back and picked up the next portion of Genesis. After that, we went back and picked up the next portion of Matthew.

This way, people are getting a well-balanced diet, both in terms of the public reading of the Word in heavy chunks and in terms of the preaching of the Word in heavy chunks and by going back and forth and connecting passages.

We did this preaching through Revelation. We started with Exodus—there's a *lot* of Exodus in Revelation—then came to Revelation. Then we went to Daniel—again, there's a *lot* of Daniel in Revelation. There are many connections between Exodus, Revelation, and Daniel. This way, our people were able to understand Exodus, Daniel, and Revelation better. We would go back and forth—a month here, a month there, six weeks here, six weeks there. This way, they were getting big, heavy doses of each of these books. Practically speaking, this caused us as a teaching team to get out of our comfort zone and preach through books we wouldn't necessarily have chosen to preach through.

Why would we commit to not only preaching books we're comfortable with? It comes from the fundamental assumption that all Scripture comes from God, that all Scripture is profitable, and that all Scripture is necessary. This forces us to deal with some of the deficiencies we had in terms of our abilities to understand and preach certain types of literature. It has been an amazing thing for our people and an amazing thing for us. Why wouldn't it be if God says in His Word that "all Scripture is breathed out by [Him]" and that all Scripture is "profitable" and necessary?

Dealing with Issues

"What about dealing with issues as they arise?" you may ask. I have two things to say about that. The first is a principle God taught us. There were many

times we were doing a verse-by-verse exposition—it was our commitment—
and something would happen that fit perfectly with the passage we were
to be preaching from! It was amazing. If our preaching ministry had been
topical, then when some political things happened, we would run to find a
passage to address it, which sounds like we're using the pulpit for a political
motive, which feels slimy. But when you're committed to the systematic
exposition of Scripture and God providentially puts you in a place where you
get to just preach what happens to be next and it goes head-on with what's
happening in the culture, then it demonstrates to people a commitment to
biblical exposition *and* to the relevance of the Bible.

There's also a second thing that happens. When we take a shotgun
approach to preaching, we tend to be more sensitive to things that are going
on; and we tend to be swayed to pick passages and topics to preach based on
what's going on. We'll be all over the place dealing with issues, and what we
end up doing is perverting the power of the pulpit and undermining our
people's ability to be fed the balanced diet they need. We're also undermining
people's confidence in not just the inerrancy but also the sufficiency of God's
Word. However, a commitment to a systematic exposition of the Word makes
us much more selective in terms of what's worth switching gears over. When
we're committed to a systematic exposition and preaching through large
portions of Scripture and we put a pin in it and go and address some other
issue, we're saying, "This issue is of tantamount importance." When we
recognize the magnitude of that kind of decision, we're a lot less likely to
switch gears over small things.

At our church, we would decide six months to a year in advance where
we're going in our preaching. We had a teaching team, and everybody would
be assigned passages to preach on. This is an incredible tool for helping young
preachers. They can listen to the rest of us handling the passages that lead
up to their assignment. And when our people know that a sermon being
preached today was planned six months to a year ago and here it is when

God's dealing right here with a pressing issue, it encourages people in terms of understanding the inerrancy and the sufficiency of God's Word.

There are times, though, when you have to switch gears. A friend of mine uses this illustration: when you are teaching and a bird flies in and perches in the room, you either address the bird in the room; or you lose the audience. Sometimes there are things that happen that are weighty, and you have to address them. For example, when Hurricane Ike came through the Houston area, our town was devastated. The following Sunday, we couldn't just walk up and carry on with the next passage as if nothing had happened. It's time to change gears and address the issue. And so we did.

We don't make a habit of doing that, though. We don't make a habit of switching sermons to fit whatever is going on out there. We commit ourselves to a balanced, healthy diet for our people and trust that God's going to give His people what they need while recognizing there are going to be moments in our culture when everything stops. Those are the times when it is important to address the issues but with the same philosophical commitment to gospel preaching. It may be a different gospel message, but it is still gospel preaching that fits whatever the occasion is. But all of this is undergirded by and built on the premise that all of the Bible is God's Word, all of the Bible is profitable, and all of the Bible is necessary. So we preach all of the Bible.

Chapter 3
Preaching with the Presence of God

Gary Wilkerson

As pastors, how do we actively invite God's presence into our preaching? Pastors who earnestly long for God's presence must decide to be crucified with Christ. When we do this, God grants us the power to carry a weight beyond our ability in a generation that needs to be carried and lifted up to the things of God.

One of the most important decisions you and I can make in our preaching is to preach Christ crucified. The apostle Paul, in his first letter to the church in Corinth, said it this way:

> And I, when I came to you, brothers, did not come proclaiming to you the testimony of God with lofty speech or wisdom. For I decided to know nothing among you except Jesus Christ and him crucified. And I was with you in weakness and in fear and much trembling, and my speech and my message were not in plausible words of wisdom, but in demonstration of the Spirit and of power, so that your faith might not rest in the wisdom of men but in the power of God (1 Cor. 2:1-5).

Paul decided what he would know and focus on. In the same way, I decide how I will disciple the people in my congregation. I decide what words I will put on the page as I write sermons. I decide what I will say. What did Paul decide? "To know nothing among you except Jesus Christ and him crucified." When we make this important decision, our faith and our life will rest not in our wisdom or eloquence but in the wisdom and the power of God.

If you were to remove the glorious, wonder-working power of God from the pulpit, what remains is only a feel-good pop psychology, a self-help talk, a motivational speech—a TED Talk, if you will. Your messages may be entertaining. They may be impressive and even emotionally stirring. But they will not be life-transforming, God-honoring, or Christ-exalting. And your messages will not be a word from Heaven. People may leave patting you on the back, saying, "I was really interested in what you had to say"; but their lives may not be transformed.

The faithful preaching of the Word of God is a supernatural act. Without supernatural power, there is no faithful preaching of the gospel. It's time we confess our lack of Divine power. It's time we acknowledge our great need for a fresh fire from Heaven to touch our lips once again and fill us with words from Heaven,[1] a heart that's on fire, and a stirring that not only stirs us as we preach but also stirs our people as they hear a fresh revelation from God.

Some of the most frightening thoughts that can strike the heart of a preacher are, *What if I have given my life to preaching, but I've only preached in my flesh? What if at the end of my days, I see it was more about me and what I wanted to say or accomplish, the applause, or the accolades I wanted rather than my preaching being something filled with the power of God?*

We must decide, as Paul did, to require a demonstration of the power of the cross of Jesus Christ—not of our skills, wisdom, or eloquence. Paul could have decided to use his background, training, education, skills, and persuasive powers. Instead, he decided he would trust in the cross of a crucified Savior.

---

1   Isaiah 6:5-7; Jeremiah 1:9-10

This was the single most important decision he made in his preaching ministry. He didn't want to be known as a scholar or scribe of the age. He didn't want to be known as one who wins debates. He wanted to be known as one who knew the things of God, the heart of God.

Have you made such a decision? Have you at any time in your life decided that you will go all out for Christ, that you will be a Christ-exalting preacher? Have you decided that you are here for Christ and not for yourself?

You have only two options. You can either make a daily choice to focus on Christ crucified, or you can choose to focus on building your own kingdom. The key is to decide. But what is it that Paul asks us to decide? First, we need to decided to be emptied of ourselves. Next, we need to decide to be weak. And finally, we need to decide to rely on the power of the Holy Spirit. Let's take a closer look at these three decisions.

Deciding to Be Emptied of Ourselves

When we choose to be emptied of ourselves, we can fully focus on the crucified Christ. And when we focus on the cross, the Holy Spirit fills our preaching with power. Our words become life-giving. They become life-transforming.

Paul makes it clear he does not use words of eloquent wisdom. In the same way, if you and I preach the gospel in our own power, eloquence, and wisdom, when we desire to be recognized for our oratory abilities and go after something other than edifying and exalting Christ, we empty the cross of its power.[2] When it comes to the division created by the fame of leaders, Paul makes it clear that Christ had sent him "to preach the gospel, and not with words of elegant wisdom, lest the cross of Christ be emptied of its power" (1 Cor. 1:17).

How is it possible for our words to make the cross of no effect to the extent that we trade the trust of God's power for trust in ourselves instead—trusting

---

2   1 Corinthians 2:4-5

in our eloquent speech, our ways with words, in how much we've studied or even prayed, how many Greek words we've translated? To that degree, we come to the pulpit in our own strength. And to that degree, we are making the power of the cross of no effect.

Sometimes, we try to sound good so that we get accolades and become sought after. When that is our focus, we operate in our own power. People leave church thinking they have heard from God, but what they heard was a motivational speech. As a result, they feel better. They feel hopeful. They may even feel like they have more faith. But it's not a godly faith. It's faith in self, in someone with clay feet. The doctrine at the heart of the message may be true. But the moment we—not God—are at the center, the message becomes powerless. That's why it is crucial for us to recognize the difference between preaching in the power of Christ and showing off our fleshly desire for power. We must know the difference between brokenhearted men and women who fall on their knees before God and those who are trying to build a brand. We need to know the difference between ego-less service and egocentric self-service.

When I was in seminary, one of my professors warned me, "When you preach, you'll always have mixed motives. Nobody preaches with a pure heart, saying, 'This is all God and none of me.' We all have a little bit of desire to be applauded and recognized."

I had felt guilty for desiring praise when I got into the pulpit. I wanted people to come up afterward and say good things about the sermon. So those words comforted me. I felt like I no longer needed to strive to be so pure in my preaching, so surrendered. I could bring a bit of myself to the pulpit. After all, we all have a fleshly nature. But this way of thinking watered down the gospel for me. It allowed me to tolerate and accept coming to the pulpit with mixed motives. Granted, I don't come to you today with completely pure motives, but I no longer accept mixed motives. I no longer tolerate any flesh in my ministry or in my preaching.

I suspect Paul knew about this, too. When he said that he sometimes does things he doesn't want to do,[3] I imagine this was also true for his preaching. Like us, Paul may have been tempted to live for fame, recognition, or a place on the stage. Like in all areas of our lives, in our preaching, we want more of Christ and less of us.[4] Otherwise, we are simply in the business of self-promotion—building a large church and fame for ourselves and an online presence or focusing on gaining followers on social media.

We can garner a following; but in doing so, our teaching will be void of the power of the gospel of Jesus Christ, void of the power available to us. Coming to church is not about being entertained; it's about receiving a word from God. That only comes from a pastor who is "crucified with Christ" (Gal. 2:20), a man or woman who preaches for the glory of Christ.

This is why Paul said, "I decided to know nothing among you except Jesus Christ and him crucified. And I was with you in weakness and in fear and much trembling, and my speech and my message were not in plausible words of wisdom, but in demonstration of the Spirit and of power" (1 Cor. 2:2-4). For this reason, I have decided that when I teach, my aim is not for somebody to say, "That was the best sermon we've ever heard!" Instead, I will deliver what God has put on my heart. My words may be weak. My appearance may be trivial. But I will be emptied of myself so what you hear ultimately are words from Heaven·

Deciding to Be Weak

The next choice we must make is to be weak. When we acknowledge we are weak, will we opt to operate in our own strength, from our own abilities, our own skills? Likely not. Instead, we will say to God, "I am totally dependent on You—not on my words nor my intellect." Acknowledging our weakness stands in stark contrast to a clamoring for recognition, using our

---

3   Romans 7:19
4   John 3:30

power to entertain, be clever, and create a wow factor at church that keeps people coming back for the lights and the smoke—not that using lights and technology is all bad. What is bad is when we use it to build our ego and our pride. That is an abomination in the sight of the Lord.

Instead, God uses "what is foolish," not "the wise" (1 Cor. 1:27). God lifts up those who are humble and opposes the proud (1 Peter 5:5). God delights in demonstrating his glorious, infinite power through weak vessels.[5] That's what God did when he freed the people of Israel from Egypt. Among other plagues, God used gnats, flies, locusts, frogs, and little hailstones to wear out Pharaoh. He could have sent giant asteroids to demonstrate his power. But he used small things to confound the wise. God showed He can use small things to do great things. Do you feel small? Do you feel inadequate? Rely on the power of God. Remember, weakness is exactly what God wants so He can demonstrate his power.

God Himself chose weakness in the coming of Jesus. He chose a humble, small-town virgin girl—likely poor, probably unknown, and insignificant—to give birth to and raise the Son of Man. God still chooses the small things to confound the wise.

The most important decision you'll ever make in your preaching ministry will be to decide, like Paul, to know nothing "except Jesus Christ and him crucified" (1 Cor. 2:2). This and only this gives you access to the power at the heart of preaching with power. Day after day, week after week, decide to preach "Christ and him crucified." It doesn't matter what anyone else brings to the pulpit. That's why Martin Luther said, "I preach the gospel to myself every day because I forget it every day."

We likewise need to preach to ourselves every day, reminding ourselves that the Bible says to deny ourselves and "take up [our] cross every day (Matt. 16:24)—especially the days we will be getting into the pulpit. The

5   1 Corinthians 1:31; 2 Corinthians 4:7

apostle Paul—despite being brilliant, having amazing leadership skills, and being extraordinary in all ways—had a decision to make. It was not a decision about the message he would preach but about the messenger. The message—the gospel—remained the same. But as the messenger, Paul chose to die to himself so that he could preach a biblical message of the cross in a way that honored God. As a preacher crucified to self, he denied himself so he could promote Christ alone.

Deciding to Rely on the Power of the Holy Spirit

We, like Paul, have another decision to make: to rely on the power of the Holy Spirit. This gives us access to a glorious reservoir of power that demonstrates the beauty, majesty, splendor, and glory of our infinitely amazing God—a God above anything we've ever known, dreamed of, or imagined. That is what you'll get to preach when you choose to be emptied of yourself—when you choose to be weak and to rely on the power of the Holy Spirit. Then God's power can be on display. You'll get to preach this God Who is high and holy and lifted up. And in doing so, God will reveal Himself to you, and you'll get to say things about God that you never even understood!

That is why Paul says that his "speech and . . . message were not in plausible words of wisdom, but in demonstration of the Spirit and of power" (1 Cor. 2:4). By choosing to be weak, Paul had access to power that comes from a dependency on the Holy Spirit. So can we. But we often wrongly expect this demonstration of power to be signs and wonders. We might preach a sermon. But at the end of the sermon, we want to pray for somebody to be healed; and that will demonstrate God's power. I believe in the healing power of the Holy Spirit. I have prayed for people and seen them healed. I will continue to do so. And God certainly gets glorified and honored in healing. But in this context here, Paul isn't speaking of the demonstration of signs and wonders. After all, he says that the Jews demand signs, but God is working against what they demand.

Instead of signs and wonders and wisdom, Christ manifests God's power and wisdom.[6] Christ *is* the Power of God. Paul, through his preaching, demonstrates that the crucified Christ has risen and is alive. He is active. In the same way, Christ is present today in our words. Christ, the exalted One, is alive today. He is still touching lives. He's still healing, saving, and demonstrating the very presence of God.

When we preach the gospel, it penetrates hardened and unrepentant hearts. God's power and presence and the conviction of the Holy Spirit change things in the atmosphere, in people's lives—even their marriages. That is what Paul is saying he wanted—a ministry where the Holy Spirit convicts people. Paul didn't want notoriety, fame, or success. Paul decided against tapping into his own power. We also can decide when we step up to preach, so what we say will change lives. It's not about us. There's something more profound, more powerful, more pressing than anything you or I could say in our own wisdom. It's about God being present among His people. It's about God speaking. It's not the oracle of philosophy or self-help but the oracle of the message of the King of kings and Lord of lords, the God of all creation, the One Who is high and lifted up.

Such a demonstration of power is required in a generation such as ours—a generation as full of darkness, lawlessness, rebellion, and sexual immorality as what Sodom had experienced in its judgment. The violence of our time, the abortion en masse, the use of legitimate drugs, and a multitude of other modern-day dilemmas will not come out by any lesser means. These can only come out through prayer and fasting.[7]

Fasting brings a man or woman to the pulpit with an ability to preach with God's power. It begins with the proclamation of the gospel, whether it be one-on-one, on the streets, in a prayer meeting, in a small group, or in the church. It begins with proclaiming that Jesus has the power to turn

---

6   1 Corinthians 1:22-24
7   Mark 9:29

a culture like that of Sodom into a culture like the kingdom of God. Jesus has the power to turn hatred into love. He has the power to turn darkness into light. He has the power to cause demons to flee. The spirits that have enslaved our generation and our nation can come out by no less a means than the gospel of a crucified, resurrected, coming-soon Christ. He has the answer for our generation.

✚

So, what do you do with this? Pause and ask yourself, *What am I chasing after? What am I longing for? Where is my heart on this topic? What are my motives?* Then decide what you will change.

Chapter 4
Preaching *for* People

Carter Conlon

Pastors filled with their own vision and successes can rarely hear anything beyond the sound of their voice. Such self-focused ministers will preach to the people. But a humble, God-focused minister will preach for the people.

As preachers, what is our calling? Is our calling driven by results? No, there is something much deeper to it. We see that in the life of Moses, whom God called to bring His people out of captivity.[1] Because of Moses's impulsiveness, anger, and lack of understanding of the ways of God, he didn't do it God's way. He did it his way. As a result, he had to flee Egypt and ended up in the wilderness for many, many years.[2] Moses thought that his calling was lost, his time in ministry had passed.

Perhaps you, too, are convinced that your season is over. You may have had a time of ministry in the strength of your youth. But now you're older; you've made mistakes along the way; and you're looking back and wondering, *How is it possible that God could still use me?*

---

1   Exodus 2-3
2   Exodus 14-Deuteronomy 31

Hear this: in your weakness, God can use you in a more powerful way than He could use you when you were at your strongest. And if you are still young, learn from Moses and those of us who have gone before you. It can save you years of frustration and heartache. It may even save you from fruitless, pointless ministry that was never ordained by God, ministry that would bear no lasting fruit.

In Exodus 3:7-10, God says to Moses:

> "I have surely seen the affliction of my people who are in Egypt and have heard their cry because of their taskmasters. I know their sufferings, and I have come down to deliver them out of the hand of the Egyptians and to bring them up out of that land to a good and broad land, a land flowing with milk and honey, to the place of the Canaanites, the Hittites, the Amorites, the Perizzites, the Hivites, and the Jebusites. And now, behold, the cry of the people of Israel has come to me, and I have also seen the oppression with which the Egyptians oppress them. Come, I will send you to Pharaoh that you may bring my people, the children of Israel, out of Egypt."

You know Moses's response, don't you? "'Who am I that I should go to Pharaoh and bring the children of Israel out of Egypt?'" (Exod. 3:11). Who am I? The calling to preach *for* people starts when you and I begin to see, hear, and know what God feels for those He loves. That is when we walk in unison with God. And there's no way we can know that until we step out of the way. In doing so, our thoughts give place to the thoughts of God and our ways to the ways of God. Then God speaks to us in a way that we can hear only by the Spirit. But a pastor filled with their own ideas, dreams, and visions can rarely hear anything beyond the sound of their voice. You will hear your own voice, and then you'll be turning to God for confirmation of your idea. It would be something you have conjured up, thinking, *This is what ministry success will look like.*

The Greatest Hindrance in Ministry

Years ago, I was preaching at a conference in Texas. During a break, a group of young pastors approached me.

One of them asked, "Pastor Carter, what is the greatest hindrance we'll face in the ministry ahead of us?"

I didn't have to pause to think of an answer. "The greatest hindrance you'll face in ministry is *you*," I told them. "Until you are out of the way, you will hinder the work of God. You will infuse it with your own ideas. You will come up with your own pathway. You will not know the heart of God. Until you get out of the way, your ministry will be frustrating. It will be a battle that you have to fight to get through. The self-focused minister will preach to the people but largely for their own success—not for the success of the people."

A ministry that doesn't preach *for* the people is high profile. It looks good. It might even have the attention of the masses. But it doesn't draw the people into the presence of God and into their inheritance.

In Matthew 23, Jesus warned the multitudes and His disciples about the scribes and the Pharisees. They were the ones who were supposed to be bringing the knowledge, presence, and ways of God to the people. They were supposed to be bringing the people back into the ways of God. And though they were preaching on the ways of God, their lives preached a different story.

For this reason, Jesus warned, "'So do and observe whatever they tell you, but not the works they do. For they preach, but do not practice. They tie up heavy burdens, hard to bear, and lay them on people's shoulders, but they themselves are not willing to move them with their finger'" (Matt. 23:3-4).

Jesus was saying that these men would be quick to instruct you on the journey, but they wouldn't take the journey themselves. They don't identify with the struggle.

That's a sad indictment of some ministries of our time. Their focus is on filling their churches with the successful, with those who can give to their cause and further their agenda. But they don't "stand at the right hand of the needy one" (Psalm 109:31). Their focus is skewed.

There's a correlation here with Jacob and Esau's encounter in Genesis 33. Remember, Jacob had stolen Esau's blessing as the firstborn son.[3] But Jacob had been touched by God[4] and had to deal with what was really in his heart. When God wrestled with Jacob, He essentially said, "You cannot obtain the blessing you desire by fraud. You cannot obtain it by pretending to be someone you're not."

The same goes for us as preachers. We cannot obtain God's blessing by talking about victory after victory in this wonderful life when we are struggling or when we're not willing to identify with the struggles of the people. That's what Jesus condemned the Pharisees for. They will tell you how to walk, but they won't walk with you. They won't share the journey with you. They're preaching to you but not for you. There is a huge difference between preaching *to* people and preaching *for* people, just like there was a marked difference in Jacob's life after God touched him.

After Jacob had given Esau gifts, "Esau said, 'Let us journey on our way, and I will go ahead of you'" (Gen. 33:12). Esau was a self-focused man. He is essentially saying, "I will take the preeminence, thank you. I will lead the parade. People will see me first. My name will receive glory."

Jacob's response is that of a man touched by God:

> "My lord knows that the children are frail, and that the nursing flocks and herds are a care to me. If they are driven hard for one day, all the flocks will die. Let my lord pass on ahead of his servant, and I will lead on slowly, at the pace of the livestock that are ahead of me and at the pace of the children, until I come to my lord in Seir" (Gen. 33:13-14).

---

3   Genesis 27
4   Genesis 32:22-32

Jacob's response is that of a leader who is *for* the people, moved by their infirmities and frailties. Such leaders recognize that they need God to walk with them every day. And if they are to represent people, they need to walk with them among them. They are kind to the poor. They go to the oppressed. They visit those in prison. They serve those who have nothing to give back.

Speaking of the scribes and Pharisees, Jesus warns that they do not fit the description of leaders who are *for* people. "They do all their deeds to be seen by others. For they make their phylacteries broad and their fringes long" (Matt. 23:5). Such leaders are very concerned about how others see them. They're obsessed with their image. They probably spend a lot of time in front of the mirror, even rehearsing how they look on stage.

Jesus continues, "And they love the place of honor at feasts and the best seats in the synagogues and greetings in the marketplaces and being called rabbi by others'" (Matt. 23:6-7).

Such leaders thrive on recognition. They thrive on being at the forefront of what's going on. They don't want to sit in the back and go unseen. They won't sit with those who are struggling. They love to teach, but they will not be taught.

I have met a lot of young ministers just like that. They love to gravitate to trends that they bring to their people, but they themselves have no ears. They cannot hear you. They are so full of their dreams, following their visions and plans, that they have no interest in hearing from others.

They preach *to* the people—not *for* the people. Their ministries are self-focused. Such ministries travel by their own strength and live by their own resources. They judge by their own standards and worship their very own religion. Their objective is self-glory. It is why they do what they do. It's all about themselves.

This has brought this nation to the brink of spiritual bankruptcy. Unless we change, we will be crying out for God to save us, just like the people of Israel did in Egypt. What we need is an influx of preachers who are *for* people.

I've never been more serious about anything that I preach to ministers in my life than I am now. Life depends on what we do and how we approach our people. God, in His mercy, has shut down a lot of ministries so that we might consider our ways, get back to biblical reality, and get back to being called of God again so that we might become ministers who do not use people as a measure of our successes.

May it be that we no longer seek to be the preeminent guest in every house or at every banquet. May we no longer care about recognition. May our hearts be for our people. And may we all take a journey that can bear much fruit for the kingdom of God and result in a huge harvest of souls in our generation.

Consider Your Motives

The prophet Isaiah says, "But this is the one to whom I will look: he who is humble and contrite in spirit and trembles at my word'" (Isa. 66:2). It doesn't matter what you or I think about whether we are successful in ministry. What matters is what God thinks when He looks at us. Are we reverently faithful to what God says? Or do we do what we do for our own glory? What are our motives?

When we stand before God one day, if our motives were impure, God won't call us good. If we haven't been faithful, He won't call us faithful. And if we haven't been servants of Him and His people, He's not going to call us a servant either.[5]

I tremble at the thought of standing before the throne of God one day, having been in a pulpit saying that I represent Him before the people if I've not been really *for* the people.

We have allowed a very light and treacherous ministry to arise in America, and it has brought us to this place where our youth are crying out for answers,

---

5   Matthew 25:23

yet they haven't considered turning to God. Oh, God, help us! Give us grace to admit our role in this.

When the people of Israel were in captivity in Babylon, Daniel opened his windows toward Jerusalem and prayed, "'To us, O Lord, belongs open shame . . . because we have sinned against you'" (Dan. 9:8). Daniel didn't exclude himself from the problem. And Moses, when God sent him to deliver the Israelites from Egypt, said to the Lord, "'Who am I . . .'" (Exod. 3:11). At one time, Moses had been royalty in the kingdom of Egypt. He had the command of an army at his disposal. He had access to the throne.

But at the time of this encounter with God in a burning bush, Moses was tending his father-in-law's sheep in the desert. I have no doubt Moses felt like a failure, that his best days were behind him. The reality, though, was that only then was he in a place where God could use him.

Because Moses recognized his failures, he could walk among the people. He was able to endure their frailties, their struggles, their trials, and their complaints.

In his weakness, in his nothingness, Moses could stand before Pharaoh, the most powerful ruler in that part of the world at the time. And with only a staff in his hand and his brother at his side, Moses could declare, "'Thus says the LORD, the God of Israel: *Let my people go, that they may hold a feast to me in the wilderness*'" (Exod. 5:1).

This was not about Moses. It was all about the people being set free to worship their God. Moses' ministry was that of intercession. He could speak the words God spoke to him. He had a word from God in his heart for Pharaoh and the people. "Let them go! They're being called of God to worship him in a place other than where they are."

Oh, God, help us! May we stand before every power of Hell and darkness with nothing but the words in our hearts that You have imparted to us. It's not about us, our ministries, our sense of who we are, or all the gimmicks and schemes that we've used in Your Name. We set it all to the side. We will stand against the evil that tries to keep every man, woman, and child in captivity.

We can speak with Your authority in our voices and our prayers, declaring, "Let the people go that they may worship God, even if their place of worship happens to be in a wilderness where they cling to You as their Provider, as their All, so that they can undertake this journey."

Step Aside So God Can Come to the Fore

Like Moses, we don't do this because of who we are but because of Who God is and the fact that He is with us. When Moses objected to God's assignment, the Lord said to Moses, "'I will be with you'" (Exod. 3:12). God will not send you and me into this generation alone. In our nothingness, frailty, failure, frustration, and wonderment, God is with us.

Like Moses, you may have started with grand visions of what your life and ministry would be, but it now seems like you're in a wilderness tending a few sheep. The truth is, only now are you ready to be used by God because the word you will be given will be from Him, not from you. There will be no more schemes about how to build a church. The Holy Spirit will give you God's plans and use you to build His church. You'll be no longer preaching *to* the people but *for* the people. It will be all about them. It will be about their freedom, healing, and usefulness in the kingdom of God.

It won't be about you anymore. But you'll be willing to fade into the background so God may come to the fore. That is the mark of the true minister of God. I've been around long enough to have seen that the one who feels the most unusable is often the one who can reach the needs of the people in their generation.

So that she could intercede for her people, Esther could not reveal she was a Jew when God appointed her to become the queen of Persia.[6] The Lord waited until Elizabeth was barren to bring forth from her womb the forerunner to Jesus Christ, John the Baptist. Elizabeth's husband, Zacharias,

---

6   Esther 1-8

had been in ministry for years while the desire to be a father was left unanswered. So when an angel appeared and told him he was going to have a son, he did not believe the angel.[7]

Likewise, David was too young,[8] Moses too old,[9] and Gideon too weak.[10] I could go on.

It seems that throughout history, when God wants to do something profound to deliver a people in a way that only He can, He searches for a man or a woman who recognizes they don't have what it takes to do the work that God is calling them to do. But they say yes for the sake of God's glory, not their own.

The same is true for us. You and I are weak. You may feel like you're at the bottom of the pile, the last person God would ever choose to do anything. But God looks to you when He wants to do something supernatural. And so you remember; and you pass along Paul's message, reminding people that God doesn't use the strong, the royal, the noble, or the wise in their own wisdom and strength. He takes those who are nobody. He takes those things that are despised by the world, and He makes them into something that we could never be so that all the glory goes back to Him.[11] God gives you a plan, and then He uses you to do something that you look back on and say, "Only God could have done this!"

Learn from Failure

Sometimes, though, you will fail. But you don't know grace until you experience failure. And you don't know God's strength and mercy until you've experienced your weakness. The greatest hindrance you'll ever face is

---

7   Luke 1:5-25
8   1 Samuel 16:5-11
9   Exodus 7:7
10   Judges 7:2-6
11   1 Corinthians 1:27-31

yourself. But until you move out of the way, you will never fully understand the power of the kingdom of God.

When you are broken and know your need for God, your ministry shifts. You start to preach for the sake of the people. Sadly, like Moses, many pastors only learn this late in life. But it's not too late for God to use you powerfully. Even if you only have a short season of ministry left, God can do more through a surrendered life—when you hear God's voice, know His heart, and understand the sorrow of the people—than He can do in many years of you relying on the strength of your youth.

It's in our weakness that you and I experience the compassion of God. And when we experience God's compassion, Christ gives us His heart for people. We become an extension of that compassion to others and preach *for* people.

Rely on the Holy Spirit

Luke tells of a time when Jesus was visiting His hometown, Nazareth, where He visited the synagogue, just as he would have done as a boy. There, Jesus was asked to read from the Scriptures, specifically from the book of Isaiah. In Luke 4:17-19, we read, "He unrolled the scroll and found the place where it was written, 'The Spirit of the Lord is upon me, because he has anointed me to proclaim good news to the poor. He has sent me to proclaim liberty to the captives and recovering of sight to the blind, to set at liberty those who are oppressed, to proclaim the year of the Lord's favor.'"

Everyone was mesmerized by this familiar passage, their eyes fixed on Jesus. So He told them in Luke 4:21, "'Today this Scripture has been fulfilled in your hearing.'" What was different about Jesus reading this passage than when they may have heard it before? Jesus was speaking for them. He had a message of hope for them and delivered it with God's heart of compassion. Soon, Jesus would release the people from captivity, just as Moses had once done, and bring them into the promise of a new and eternal life. He wouldn't do it with the strength of an army. He would do it in the weakness of the cross. Their freedom could not be gained by the hands of men—only by the hand of God.

Jesus declared that the Spirit of the Lord was upon Him to fulfill the ministry for which He was sent. How about you? How can you and I lay claim to having the Spirit of God resident within us if we don't care about the poor? What if God told you, "I'm making you a minister to the poor. I will fill this house with men, women, and children who have nothing to contribute financially, simply because I love them. I died for them. And I know I can entrust them to your care"? You love them. You walk with them through their struggles and lead them to the place of God's promised provision for their lives.

As for the brokenhearted, those who live in captivity to the spirit of the world, and those who cannot see a way forward, you help them find an understanding of the ways and the will of God so that they can see the way forward. Will you do that? Will you help them to lay hold of God's plan for their lives? And like John the Baptist, will you step away when Jesus shows up and say, "Look! There is the Lamb of God! Follow *Him*, not me! My ministry is merely to point you toward Him."[12] We can do that if our hearts are *for* God's people. You might not be fully there yet, but may you and I declare today, "I am willing for God to place that kind of love in my heart. I am willing to die to my plans, dreams, and ambitions of what ministry even is."

---

12   John 1:29-34

Chapter 5
Preaching and Preparation

Tim Dilena

What practical and spiritual steps can you take to prepare life-changing sermons? Beginning at the right points in your preparation can exponentially increase your effective communication. Such starting points might not be intuitive, but they are incredibly important.

In his commentary on the book of Acts, Kent Hughes points out that the Greeks were known for their excellent communication skills. They believed for you to speak with authority and effectiveness, you needed three things at work in your life. First, you need *logos*. You had to have content with depth, something that has been studied well. For us, it is the written Scriptures, the Bible. Next, you need *ethos*, which is character. You must live the content you're preaching to be effective. If not, you're sabotaging your message. The third thing the Greeks said you need is *pathos*. You need passion. You need to be moved by your message.[1]

Even in your preparation, you must understand how important *logos*, *ethos*, and *pathos* are for you to communicate effectively. Preparing to preach is not just about preparing a sermon; it's about preparing your life.

---

1   R. Kent Hughes, *Acts: The Church Afire (Preaching the Word)* (Wheaton: Crossway, 2014).

In Matthew 13, Jesus tells a series of parables about the kingdom of Heaven. Among those, Jesus says, "'[T]he kingdom of heaven is like treasure hidden in a field, which a man found and hid; and for joy over it he goes and sells all that he has and buys that field. [And] the kingdom of heaven is like a merchant seeking beautiful pearls, who, when he had found one pearl of great price, went and sold all that he had and bought it'" (vs. 44-46).

In these two short parables, we're dealing with preparation. In the first, a man was working in a field when he accidentally found a treasure. In the second, the man knew that there was a pearl of great value, and he deliberately looked for it. As you prepare to preach the Word of God, be like the second man who has his tools ready to find a treasure. Ask God to give you the right type of tools, so you can find those pearls of great value.

Tools for Sermon Preparation

In preparing for sermons, there are several tools I have used in the almost forty years I've been preaching. These have been trusted friends to me, helping me to find pearls of great value.

1. Collect Good Quotes.

The first tool I use is to collect quotes from preachers and speakers over the centuries. I keep a list of good quotes in my journal to remind me what I'm getting ready to do. These quotes keep me grounded. I'll share several throughout this chapter, but one by C. S. Lewis stands out for now. "'Odd,' he said, 'the less the Bible is read, the more it is translated.'"[2] This reminds me that when I don't consume the Bible myself, I will be leaning on shaky ground, simply interpreting passages and not living them.

---

2   C. S. Lewis, *Mere Christianity* (San Francisco: Harper San Francisco, 2001).

2. Follow a Bible-Reading Plan.

To prepare to be an effective preacher, I read through the entire Bible at least once a year. I've been using a Bible-reading plan from Scottish preacher Robert Murray M'Cheyne for years.[3] If you follow M'Cheyne's plan, you'll read through the Old Testament once and the New Testament twice in one year. This allows you to look at the logos not simply as short passages or as portions within the narrative of a chapter; but you are mindful of the metanarrative, the whole picture of what God is saying from Genesis through Revelation.

When you don't read the Bible, it is easy to lean upon denominational values instead of upon what God says through His Word. It's also easy to take a verse out of context to drive home your point. And when you rob a verse of its context, you rob it of the power of the truth. When you regularly read through the whole Bible, though, you see the consistency of God's voice— God's love, mercy, compassion, wrath, and nature. It also keeps you mindful not to use verses out of context simply to make a point.

3. Read Good Theology.

German theologian Karl Barth said, "Theology is the conscience of preaching."[4] Bearing this in mind, I try to read one systematic theology book every year to challenge myself to see what people throughout the centuries have said about the nature and the character of God and about soteriology and eschatology.

Theology is the study of God. Reading good theology keeps our preaching centered. God becomes the focus of our preaching. That's why I agree with Dr. Martyn Lloyd-Jones from Westminster Chapel, who said, "Preaching is theology on fire." But you should only read those books to "check your work," just like

---

3   See https://bibleplan.org/plans/mcheyne.
4   Karl Barth, *Church Dogmatics* (Peabody: Hendrickson Publishers, 2010).

you can check your solutions to problems from the back of a math book. If you do math relying just on those answers, you never learn how to do it. Reading theology books more than you read the Bible is dangerous in the same way.

4. Pray.

Another quote I love is from Martin Luther, who said, "He who has prayed well has studied well." There is a big difference between a well-studied sermon and a well-prayed-over sermon. It's a difference of authority. When you pray over a message as part of the preparation, it takes that truth and makes it timely truth. It makes it personal truth. That's the power of prayer in our preparation.

5. Preach from Your Devotional Life.

When I'm getting ready to preach, I also lean on what A. W. Tozer said: "If we've read the Bible but haven't encountered the Living Word, then we haven't really read the Bible."[5] It's important to remember that when I'm reading through the Scriptures every day, I'm there to encounter God, not to find something for a sermon. It keeps me steadied to think, *I want to meet you, God. These are Your words. There are people throughout the centuries who couldn't even hold the Bible without it being a death threat upon their lives. But I have the living Word of God in my hands. Now, let me meet the Living Word, Jesus. Let me encounter You as I read Your Word.*

Someone once asked me, "What's the greatest thing you've learned in almost four decades of preaching?"

It's such a broad question, but I knew the answer immediately. I told him, "I've learned to preach from my devotional life, not from studying for a sermon."

When I'm in the Word of God, searching for "the pearls of great price," I'm not searching for a sermon. I'm searching for God to touch me. In doing so, the *logos* turns to *ethos* as God is working in me. And when God's working

---

5   A. W. Tozer, *The Pursuit of God* (Abbotsford: Aneko Press, 2015).

in me, the *pathos* comes. That's when a passage goes from being words on a page and becomes a sermon.

6. Allow the Bible to Defend Itself.

When someone asked C. H. Spurgeon to defend the Bible as the Word of God, Spurgeon said, "Suppose a number of persons were to take it into their heads that they had to defend a lion, full-grown king of beasts!"[6] The Bible will defend itself. That's why when I have a chance to do a devotional for anybody outside of the church, I have two rules: I will preach the Bible, and I will lift up Jesus. Why do I do that? The Bible promises that the "word will not return . . . void" (Isa. 55:11). And it promises if Jesus be lifted up, He will draw all men to him.[7]

Let the lion out of the cage; let the Lion of Judah roar. It can defend itself. When you lift up Jesus, He is more attractive than any personality standing in the pulpit, any personality holding a microphone. In fact, one preacher said it like this: "When men are clever, then Jesus is not wonderful."

You and I have a responsibility to lift up the name of Jesus, to let the lion out of the cage by reading the passage and letting the truth of God go to people's hearts and change their nature.[8]

7. Be Generous with the Time You Spend with God.

J. C. Ryle reminds us, "No one has ever said at the end of his life, 'I've read my Bible too much, I thought of God too much, and I prayed too much.'"[9] Some people try to take the Bible, prayer, and preparation and say, "I want quality, not quantity." Quantity is not even an issue. The more I do it, the

---

6   Charles Haddon Spurgeon, "Christ and His Co-Workers" (sermon, Metropolitan Tabernacle Pulpit Volume 42, June 10, 1886), https://www.spurgeon.org/resource-library/sermons/christ-and-his-co-workers/#flipbook/.

7   John 12:32

8   Isaiah 55:10-13

9   J. C. Ryle, *Repentance: What It Means to Repent and Why We Must Do So* (Abbotsford: Aneko Press, 2021).

more I'm blessed. In other words, you will never not be profited by spending much time in the Word.

8. Borrow Insights from Others.

Spurgeon also famously said, "He who will not use the thoughts of other men's brains proves that he doesn't have any brains of his own."[10] This is not about plagiarism; it's about relying upon people who have labored and taken deliberate journeys to find pearls of great value. Be careful, though, not to just copy and paste others' words. Not only is it plagiarism, but you also go from *logos* to sermon, and you lose the *ethos* and *pathos*. It leaves you with a message with no real life-changing power.

A Process for Developing a Sermon

My process of writing a sermon starts with the Bible, with God speaking through His Word. From there, God gives me revelation, a principle that speaks to me. Next, the illustration is how the principle speaks to life. And the action step speaks to the people. Here is how you can use this process:

1. Listen for a Verse.

As you read the Word devotionally, pay attention when a verse sticks out or stays with you. You'll see the *logos* in that verse, which stirs a desire for this truth to be part of your life—that's the *ethos*. Then the *pathos* kicks in. There's something here. This is God speaking.

One pastor says it like this: "The preacher is not a chef, he's a waiter. God doesn't want you to make the meal, he just wants you to deliver it to the table

---

10   Charles Haddon Spurgeon, "Paul—His Cloak and His Books" (sermon, Metropolitan Tabernacle Pulpit Volume 9, November 29, 1863).

without messing it up."[11] This isn't your word or my word; it's God's Word. We've got to just deliver it the way that God said it.

2. Listen for Revelation

Once you feel *pathos* over the verse, God will give you a thought or revelation that stirs that passion and challenges your character. Nobody can give you passion. It's something God stirs in your heart. And that is where truth becomes timely truth—truth for the moment. The verse pops off the page, and God gives you a thought. He gives revelation. Using that principle God is speaking to you, your mind starts to work.

3. Find the Right Illustration.

Next, you can ask, "God, how can I communicate this to people? How can I make it understandable? How can I illustrate this principle?" This illustration becomes the connection to the people to whom you're speaking. It's about connecting the verse with the principle—the thought or revelation—God has given you. This is what speaks to real life and where it gets clear.

4. Identify the Action Step.

Once you have the verse, the revelation, and the illustration, it leads you to the action step, the challenge. This is where you go from ears to heart—from your heart to their heart. If the *logos* and the *ethos* are living in you, *pathos* becomes the currency that gets the revelation from your heart to their heart. But for the principle to live on in people's lives, there must be an action step they can take so their lives can be changed. This is the challenge for those who are listening to do something practical, not simply listen to a sermon.

---

11   John MacArthur, "Principles for an Effective Missionary, Part 1," Grace to You, June 7, 1981, https://www.gty.org/library/sermons-library/2277.

Following these four steps is not sufficient for developing a sermon, though. The next practical tool for preparation and preaching—for seeking and presenting a pearl of great value—is exegesis and homiletics.

Using Good Exegesis and Homiletics

Exegesis is the study of a passage, and homiletics is the preaching. Proper exegesis helps you find God's voice in the Scriptures and not put words in God's mouth, claiming a verse says something that it doesn't say. That is why it must be done right. This is a very important part of preparation, even before we get into the preaching part, homiletics.

If you have poor exegesis, it doesn't matter how good of a speaker you are. People can clap; but if your exegesis is messed up, God will not applaud you. And God is the only audience that counts. Doing good exegesis is the best chance for good homiletics. Good study helps set us up for good preaching. There is danger, though. I know great exegetes who are poor at homiletics. They cannot preach. They can study a passage and pull out the voice of God, but they don't know how to communicate it.

I also know great preachers who are terrible at exegesis. They are just entertainers. Unless you do both exegesis and homiletics well, you're either boring or an entertainer. You must do both well if you want to communicate the greatest message ever told. It's a horrific crime to take the greatest story ever told and make it boring, cloudy, or unintelligible. This is the challenge for us as preachers. We must be good at exegesis, *and* we must be good at homiletics. But to do that, we must be deliberate. We must have some more tools to go on that journey.

So far, I showed you how the ancient Greeks saw *logos*, *ethos*, and *pathos* as key ingredients for excellent communication. But there's also a verse from the Hebrew king, Solomon, who, next to Jesus, was the wisest man who has ever walked the planet. This verse has been one of the most important verses in terms of helping me in my preaching. Solomon had sought to find delightful words, to capture truth as proverbs. This verse is from his diary, the book of Ecclesiastes, where he talks about communication, saying, "Besides being wise, the Preacher also taught the people knowledge, weighing and studying and arranging many proverbs with great care. The Preacher sought to find words of delight, and uprightly he wrote words of truth. The words of the wise are like goads, and like nails firmly fixed are the collected sayings; they are given by one Shepherd" (Eccl. 12:9-11).

This is probably one of the most powerful passages on exegesis and homiletics. The exegesis lies in this: the preacher *weighed* and *studied* wisdom. Next comes the homiletics: He arranged those words as proverbs; he found *words of delight*, and he wrote words that were *true*. What Solomon is saying is that if you do exegesis right, then when you preach, it would be like "goads" and "nails firmly fixed" in the lives of the people to whom you're teaching. In this passage, Solomon is showing us how to go from the text to the sermon, how to go from the Bible to the pulpit.

Learning Good Exegesis from King Solomon

1. Ponder God's Word.

Pondering God's Word is not about getting through a chapter. When you ponder the Word of God, you slow down to see what God is saying. You listen to the heart of God. You can do this by using meditation and repetition.

2. Discover Meditation.

You may be following a Bible-reading plan; but when the Holy Spirit highlights something, meditation is about just staying put. It's not about moving on quickly to get to the rest of the day's reading but pausing instead and asking, *God, what are You saying to me? What do You want me to do here?* You see what the *logos* is. You feel like God is challenging you with *ethos*. Once the *logos* starts working, the *pathos* begins to come.

When the Holy Spirit highlights something, pause. Don't go any further. Don't try to finish the day's reading just to get your chapters in. Pause—and if there's something you want to write down, write. Words breed more words and thoughts. So, write. Keep writing. Even if there is no moment of pause during your reading, commit to writing down something about what you've read. It could be a question. It could be a thought. It could be a revelation.

That is what I mean by meditation. It's not some weird Eastern thing. It's just saying, "God, You're pausing here. I feel something. Let me just see what You're saying. Let me just write."

3. Try Repetition.

Repetition is another way you can ponder on the Word of God. There have been times when, after reading my four chapters from the Bible-reading plan, I would go to one of the smaller books of the Bible and read the entire book every day for a month and ponder what the Holy Spirit is highlighting through repetition.

There was a season when God had given me revelation around the prayers Peter and John had prayed during a time of persecution. Jesus prayed on the cross, and Jonah prayed in the belly of a whale.[12] They had all quoted prayers from the psalms during their times of greatest need. So I went on a journey of repetition. I read five psalms each day, which meant I read through the psalms in a month. I did this for two years. This repetition gave me a language in prayer. It gave me a go-to when I was going through difficult times.

4. Search Out the Meaning.

Pondering, meditation, and repetition lead to searching out the meaning of the Scriptures. This is where tools come in, such as looking up the meaning in the ancient languages. There are many great online tools today that give you access to the Hebrew and Greek meanings, whether you studied those in

---

12   Acts 4; Matthew 27:46; Mark 15:34; John 19:30; Jonah 2

the past and have forgotten all you had learned or whether you have never studied the ancient languages. You can also search out more of what the Holy Spirit highlights by turning to commentaries and theological books to help dig to find those pearls of great value.

One of the greatest study tools for me has been The Treasury of Scripture Knowledge.[13] It takes a passage from the Bible, breaks it up, and cross-references phrases from that passage to other passages in the Bible. It contains more than half a million cross-references!

There's no better explanation of the Word of God than the Word of God. It's the Bible explaining the Bible. Nothing is more powerful than when you let the Bible explain itself instead of putting words in God's mouth. That's good exegesis, saying, "This is what God says, not what I'm saying."

5. Learn Good Homiletics from King Solomon.

Once you've done the exegesis, you've got to get to homiletics. You've got to preach. Solomon gave us this structure for teaching. He said he *arranged* many proverbs, sought the right words (*words of delight*), and *wrote words of truth.*

To arrange words is to have structure and an outline. It's about giving understanding, not just speaking from the hip. This is literally saying, *Help me, God, to add structure to what You're saying. Help me to have a flow to what You're saying so that I'm not just speaking randomly.* I love that Solomon uses the word "arranged" to make sure that the thoughts flow from the introduction to the conclusion. By arranging the words well, you present one or two big thoughts that people can follow instead of just speaking randomly.

Next, Solomon says you must find "words of delight." You must find the right words to make a message come alive. You must find words that people can connect with so the message makes sense to them. This can come in the form of an application or an illustration. Your job and mine is to take

---

the ancient text and make it relevant to today's issues. You cannot have an application without timeless truth. That goes back to why it's critical for us to identify the timeless truth of what God is saying through good exegesis.

As for using an illustration, one of the ancient proverbs says, "The best speaker can turn the ears into eyes." That's what illustration does. It makes it memorable. It makes it stick.

It is the way Jesus spoke. Jesus was never without a story; He was never without an illustration when He spoke.[14]

Think about it. Can you tell me the story of the prodigal son but pick it up from the pigpen? Of course, you can. The son comes to his senses and goes home, and the father runs to meet him. Why did you remember those details? Those "words of delight," the illustration, made it stick.

Your sermon might have several good points, but people aren't going to remember point three or four. But they will remember the illustration. This takes work, though, because it's not about entertaining the audience with stories. It's about you deciding that you want them to get this. As Spurgeon said, "You must attract fish to your hook. And if they don't bite, it's not the fish that have the problem. It's the fisherman that has the problem."[15] If they're not biting, don't yell at the congregation. Don't yell at those hearers. It comes back to you and me.

Finally, Solomon says to write the upright truth. Make it simple; make it understandable. Do not confuse people with your message. John Wesley, one of the greatest preachers on two continents in the nineteenth century, would literally practice his sermons with his household help, not the elites. Then he would ask them, "Did you understand? Was it simple enough?" What he was saying was, "I'm the fisherman. If people aren't biting, I'm the problem."

---

14   Mark 4:34
15   Charles Spurgeon, "The Sword and the Trowel" (sermon, Tabernacle Prayer Meeting, September 1878).

One of the greatest compliments I've received over the years is when children come up to me and say, "Pastor Tim, I liked when you said that. I remember what you said today."

That means the world to me because if a child can get it, I'm doing my job. I'm doing what I'm supposed to do: from the structure to the right words, I am making it as simple as I can.

Solomon says the goal of all the pondering, searching out meaning, arranging words, finding the right words, and making the message understandable is that you get to the goad. In the New Testament, the apostle Paul talked about it in his conversion. "'Saul, Saul, why are you persecuting me? It is hard for you to kick against the goads'" (Acts 26:14). In Paul's conversion, Jesus was the Goad. A goad is a spiked stick to make an ox go in the right direction. It stimulates action. It gets the animal to move onto the right path.

This is what Solomon is saying: get your exegesis and your homiletics right. Ponder, search out wisdom. Make sure you're not putting words in God's mouth and that you're saying what God is saying. Then arrange those words, find the right words, and say them simply and plainly. Then, he says, your message will get people going in the right direction.

Jim Elliott gives us great advice. He was a martyr in Ecuador in the 1950s, but he's also known for the discipline of his devotional life. In dealing with being a preacher, Elliot said, "I must no longer depend on pleasant impulses to get me before the Lord to study and to pray. I have to respond to principles I know to be right, whether I feel them to be enjoyable or not."[16] In other words, you must be driven to get this right, so you can make sure you're sending people in the right direction.

Even Solomon understands that when you get the *logos* and the *ethos*, the *pathos* comes. And to me, his words around exegesis and homiletics become

---

16   Elizabeth Elliott, *Shadow of the Almighty: The Life and Testament of Jim Elliot, in Lives of Faith* (New York: Harper Collins, 2009).

a tool for preparing to teach the Word of God so you and I can be effective in finding and sharing pearls of great value.

Chapter 6
Preaching and Presentation

Voddie T. Baucham, Jr.

Passion and natural skill in public speaking can only take a preacher so far.
You also need a deep commitment to the biblical text to preach with true
power and authority. This way, you can develop sermons in line with the Bible
and alive with the power of God's truth.

Preaching is an art and a science. Unfortunately, a lot of pastors lean in one direction or the other. When you are a gifted communicator, for example, you may tend to lean hard on the art of preaching and not so much on the science. When you do that, your content may be persuasive; but it's compromised. That's how people get led off into error. When you are a persuasive individual but you have compromised content, you're emphasizing the art, not the science.

On the other side, you might emphasize the science of preaching and not the art. In that instance, you can have amazing content; but nobody wants to listen. Not only is your sermon not connecting with people, but you are also communicating that God is just there for us to know intellectually, not spiritually and experientially. We want to marry the art and science of preaching by taking a journey from text to sermon.

When I talk about the journey from text to sermon, I'm talking about how to get from a passage of Scripture to an organized, persuasive, Christ-centered, gospel-centered sermon. Wayne McDill, in his book *12 Essential Skills for Great Preaching*, writes, "The building of a bridge is an apt metaphor for the interpretation challenge we face as preachers. We look across the chasm between our own day and that of the biblical writers. For the sake of our hearers, we must cross to the other side and bring back the message once delivered to those ancient believers."[1]

As pastors, that's what we're doing. We don't just go to a biblical passage and read and cite the passage. We must go over into another world, culture, and time. There's a different language, people, time, and region. Everything's different on the other side of the bridge in the world in which the passage was written. We must go into the original setting and bring something back that is useful for those who are listening to us.

The challenge of going from text to sermon lies in mapping a course for crossing the bridge. And on this map, we're going to follow a roadway.

Start with God

God is the ultimate Author of the passages. The original message comes from God, so we start with God. God is the One Who communicates this message to and through the biblical author. This message passes through the original Author to us. And through the sermon, we as preachers communicate that message to our audience.

This is a three-tiered process. As you go from text to sermon, you must be aware of all three of these layers. You don't just start at the bottom with you and your audience. If there's an issue in your church, you may be tempted to go hunting for a text from the Bible so you can address the issue. In doing so, you're starting from the bottom up. You're going backward. You're looking for a text to address an issue; and then you preach it in a way that you're putting

---

1   Wayne McDill, *12 Essential Skills for Great Preaching* (Nashville: B&H Academic, 2018).

it at God's doorstep when, ultimately, it originated with you. Do you see the problem with that?

Unfortunately, that is the way a lot of people preach. They start with themselves, their people, and something they want to communicate; and then they go looking for a text in the Bible to support their idea. Instead, we must start with God, the original Messenger, Who communicated His message to and through the apostles and prophets, who then communicated through the Bible to us so we can communicate to our hearers.

We must start with the assumption that God knows what his people need better than we do. If you don't believe that, then you won't start with God. If you don't believe that, you'll use God as a means to an end instead of seeing God as the ultimate end. But if you start with the assumption that God knows what His people need, you will want what God has for you, and you will want to communicate to your people what God has for you. To do that effectively, you must map a course.

Map a Course

In the first three steps of mapping the course, you're on the other side of the bridge, looking at what the author is saying in the original passage.

The verse you're looking at comes in a context. You must identify connections within that context that contribute to its meaning. In other words, when you're looking at a passage of Scripture, you have to remember that this passage of Scripture is part of a bigger section of Scripture. This bigger section of Scripture may be part of a chapter. This chapter is part of a book.

Let's say I'm looking at a verse in Philippians 2. This verse is part of a paragraph. And that paragraph is part of a section. That section is part of the chapter. That chapter is part of the book of Philippians. The book of Philippians is part of the Pauline literature. The Pauline literature is part of the epistles. The epistles are part of the New Testament. The New Testament is part of the Bible. The Bible is part of the overall message that God has revealed to us.

Once you understand that a verse comes in that context, pay attention to the structure of the text. Outline the author's organization of a passage to show that structure. There are a lot of ways that you can do that. For simplicity's sake, let's just say you can use book outlines.

Ultimately, though, you want to do an outline of the structure so you can get into the text and get to the author's meaning.

Notice that you haven't started talking about writing the sermon yet. A lot of times, we jump to saying, "I want to preach a sermon, and I want my sermon to have this theme."

Resist the temptation to do that. Instead, ask what the theme of the text is within its context. Your theme will come from the text. Your theme will come as a direct result of you looking at the biblical text in its biblical context and asking, "What is this text about?" You're not writing a sermon yet. You're just understanding the text.

Next, look at the aim of the text. You get to the aim by asking, *What is this text trying to accomplish?*

In the next step, you combine the theme and the aim you had identified so you can get to the central proposition of this passage and communicate the author's point in a single statement. I'll provide an example of that later in this chapter.

On this journey across the bridge, it is now time for you to turn around so you can come to your audience. You do this by identifying connections in the passage to the person and work of Christ. We preach Christ. We preach the gospel. We preach the good news of the Person and the work of Christ. So, you must ask how this relates to the overall message of the Bible, which is about Christ, His person, and His work. How does this text connect to the Person and the work of Christ?

In light of these connections to Christ that you had identified in step four, restate the central proposition from step three in terms of our audience.

Next, state the application that you would make to your audience from this passage.

Mapping a Course: From Text to Sermon

Context | *What is the context of this passage?*

Structure | *How is it structured?*

Theme | *What is this text about?*

Aim | *What is this text trying to accomplish?*

Central Proposition | *How can I communicate the author's point in a single statement?*

Christ Connection | *How does this text relate to the Person and the work of Christ?*

Restate Proposition | *In light of the gospel, how can I communicate the author's point?*

Application | *How can I apply this to my hearers?*

So, you start on one side of the bridge in the ancient text. You look at the text, context, structure, theme, aim, and central proposition. Only then do you cross back over to the contemporary side of the bridge and try to communicate what you have found in the ancient text by working toward a sermon.

First, identify the "fallen condition" focus. Bryan Chapell says, "Until we have determined a passage's purpose, we are not ready to preach its truth, even if we know many true facts about the text. Yet as obvious as this is, it is frequently neglected. Preachers often think they're ready to preach when they see a doctrinal subject reflected in a passage, though they have not yet determined the text's specific purpose.[2]

---

2   Bryan Chapell, *Christ-Centered Preaching: Redeeming the Expository Sermon* (Ada: Baker Academic, 2018).

For example, simply recognizing that a passage contains features that support the doctrine of justification by faith alone does not adequately prepare a pastor to preach. A sermon is not just a systematics lesson. We must determine the purpose or burden of a passage before we really know the subject of a sermon. This goes back to the idea of the aim of a passage. The passage is not just there to communicate a doctrinal truth hanging in the air, if you will. The passage is there to communicate a doctrinal truth for a purpose.

Each passage has a burden, as Chapell says here; and to get to and understand that burden, we must look at what he calls the fallen-condition focus. Chapell describes it: "The fallen condition focus is the mutual human condition that contemporary believers share with those for or by whom the text was written that requires the grace of the passage to manifest God's glory in his people."[3]

This condition is mutual. People in the ancient world, place, and time share this fallen condition with us as contemporary believers. If I'm reading the passage from Philippians, there is a common or mutual human condition that I share not only with Paul's audience but also with Paul as well. We must identify that mutual human condition we share, the condition "that requires the grace of the passage to manifest God's glory in his people."

Don't miss this! If you do, your sermons could be preached as how-to seminars. They could be preached in a mosque or in a Jewish temple, and nobody would be offended because you're not preaching Christ. So-called sermons on "Five Steps to Have a Happy Life" or "Four Ways to Reduce Stress" don't get to the heart of the matter. Anyone can listen to messages like those! Pagans can listen and not be confronted with the gospel nor with their need for a Savior.

But when you understand that man is fallen, you are fallen, the original author is fallen, and your audience is fallen and that this truth was communicated to address us in our fallenness and to apply God's grace to us

---

3   Chapell.

in our fallenness for His glory through the Person and the work of Christ, now, all of a sudden, you're preaching the gospel.

This message would no longer fly in a mosque or a Jewish synagogue because we understand God's answer to our fallen condition lies in the cross of Christ. When you're preparing a sermon, ask yourself, *Is this something that would fly at the Rotary Club? Is this something that would be fine if I taught it at a synagogue?* If it is, then you're not preaching the gospel. You're just giving a how-to seminar. You're doing pop psychology from the pulpit. You're not preaching Christ.

So, how do you find that? How do you identify that fallen condition focus? There are four angles: anthropological, Christological, soteriological, and doxological.

The anthropological view starts with the text to identify the contemporary need for grace that we share with the original audience. Look at the text from an anthropological angle to identify human needs by asking these three questions:

- *What does the text say?* Here is where you're doing your work in the text. You're doing word studies, diagrams, outlines, grammatical studies, and looking at the background so you can get to what the text says. You're not doing what most modern Bible studies do. You read a verse and then go around the room and ask, "What does this mean to you?" I don't care what it means *to you.* I want to know what it really means.
- *What are its concerns?* As you're reading a passage, ask, in light of the context, what the concerns are that the passage addresses.
- *What are the commonalities?* What do listeners spiritually have in common with those for or about whom it was written or the one by whom it was written? Here, you're getting to the mutuality with the ancient writer and his audience.

Next is the Christological View. Here, you're looking at Christ. The focus is on Christ. Christ *must* be the Link between the text and the sermon. Christ must be the Link between one side of the bridge and the other. Christ is the Answer. If Christ is not the answer to whatever the problem is that you found, you either identified the wrong problem; or you have the wrong answer. There's just one question to ask at this step of your work: *What aspect of the Person and the work of Christ is highlighted in the text?*

It won't always be Christ on this cross. Here, you're not just talking about Jesus's death, burial, and resurrection. It may be some other aspect of the Person and work of Christ. This is often the case when you're dealing with the Old Testament narratives. You may be looking at a type of Christ, like David or Moses. You may be looking at a foreshadowing of Christ in the sacrifice of Isaac, for example, in Christ as that lamb. Or you may be looking at the need for Christ in the book of Judges as those judges fail over and over and over again. They don't have the ultimate answer Israel needs. That points us to the fact that there is a Judge to come Who will ultimately address that need.

Insofar as the soteriological angle to exploring the text goes, the focus is on God and how God meets the human need for a Savior. How does the grace of the passage manifest God's glory in His people and God's glory in saving His people and rescuing us from our sins?

Finally, the doxological view focuses on the praise we offer God because He, and He alone, meets our need. Here, you ask, *How and why can we give glory to God for the grace He has bestowed?* If you're offering pop psychology from the pulpit, these focuses won't all show up in your message. There may be an anthropological focus, but neither the Christological focus nor the soteriological focus is going to be there. And then the doxological focus will be on us humans because we were able to do the simple steps proclaimed in the message.

Writing a Sermon

Finally, there are three important concepts I've alluded to and want to explain more here: the text idea, the sermon idea, and a purpose statement. Then we'll get to your sermon points and, finally, to writing a sermon.

To get to a text idea, there are two important concepts you must first identify: the subject (*What is the author's main topic, truth, or concept?*) and the modifier (*What is the author saying about that main topic, truth, or concept?*) Let's look at this using 2 Timothy 1:8-14:

> Therefore do not be ashamed of the testimony about our Lord, nor of me his prisoner, but share in suffering for the gospel by the power of God, who saved us and called us to a holy calling, not because of our works but because of his own purpose and grace, which he gave us in Christ Jesus before the ages began, and which now has been manifested through the appearing of our Savior Christ Jesus, who abolished death and brought life and immortality to light through the gospel, for which I was appointed a preacher and apostle and teacher, which is why I suffer as I do. But I am not ashamed, for I know whom I have believed, and I am convinced that he is able to guard until that day what has been entrusted to me. Follow the pattern of the sound words that you have heard from me, in the faith and love that are in Christ Jesus. By the Holy Spirit who dwells within us, guard the good deposit entrusted to you.

There are several subjects discussed in this passage: suffering, proclaiming, preserving, and partnering. But the subject must have a modifier. If we chose *suffering* as the subject, then *purposeful* could be the modifier. We see that in Paul saying, "Therefore do not be ashamed of the testimony about our Lord, nor of me his prisoner, but share in suffering for the gospel by the power of God." There is a purpose to his suffering. That's not the only subject with a modifier that you could see from this passage; but if you're going to preach a sermon, choose just one subject and modifier per sermon.

There's more to the text idea than just a subject and a modifier, though. McDill describes a text idea as "a clear, precisely worded sentence that concisely states the idea of the text writer."[4]

For a good text idea:

- Include the writer, speaker, key character, and statement
- Note the purpose of the writer or tone of the text in the statement
- Refer to secondary characters, hearers, or readers
- Consider the occasion of writings, the situation, or circumstances
- Include any literary features relevant to the meaning of the text.

Using the passage from Timothy and putting this together, here's an example of a text idea: *Paul called Timothy to join him in suffering for the sake (purpose) of preserving and proclaiming the gospel.* There is suffering, and there is purpose. What's the purpose of suffering? Preserving and proclaiming the gospel. That's still not my sermon. That's just me getting the text idea.

Now that I have the text idea, I need to get the sermon idea. The text idea is what Paul said to Timothy. But what about what I'm saying to my audience? I've got to get back across the bridge. McDill describes the sermon idea as "a universal principle that applies to everyone who might hear it instead of a particular message to the writer's audience."[5]

Remember, this is that same focus—the fallen condition focus. They're fallen; we're fallen. What's this common fallenness that we have? And how does this text address it dealing with the same thing here? We're looking for that universal principle. We're trying to universalize this here. Again, using the passage from Paul's letter to Timothy and putting it all together, here's an example of a sermon idea: *Christians are called to join in suffering for the sake of preserving and proclaiming the gospel.*

---

4   McDill.
5   McDill.

Do you see the difference between the examples? This is no longer just about Timothy. This is universal. Now when you're preaching based on this sermon idea, the person in the pew doesn't have the luxury of just sitting there and saying, "Oh, this is a history lesson about what Paul said to Timothy." Instead, they're hearing a universal truth that applies to everyone who calls on the name of Christ. We've come across the bridge, and we brought back that universal truth. We've restated it in the sermon idea.

Table 1: The Difference Between Text Idea and the Sermon Idea

• What the text writer said	• What the preacher is saying
• Based on the subject and modifier	• Based on the subject and modifier
• Written as a complete sentence	• Written as a complete sentence
• A historical statement	• A timeless truth
• Of a particular occasion	• Of a universal principle
• A theological concept	• A theological concept
Example: Paul called Timothy to join him in suffering for the sake of preserving and proclaiming the gospel.	*Example: Christians are called to join in suffering for the sake of preserving and proclaiming the gospel.*

Once you have a sermon idea, it is time to create a purpose statement. A sermon must have a purpose, and the purpose of the sermon is not just to communicate some information or fill some time. Again, we turn to Wayne McDill for insight. He says, "Another way to think of the sermon purpose is to project what the audience response might be to the specific message of the sermon."[6] Here, you ask, *What do I want my audience to do with this?*

---

6   McDill.

This gets you away from dry exegetical history lessons in the pulpit. What do you want your audience to *do*? It's not just about what you want them to learn but what you want them to do. You're getting away from this being far off somewhere, and you're crawling up into people's seats with this. An example of a purpose statement from the text: *I want to see Christians prize and pursue the proclamation of the gospel so dearly that they willingly embrace the suffering that doing so will bring.*

Now only do you get to writing the sermon points. Do not do this when you start out writing a sermon. Do not do this and then come back and look for verses to help support your points. You do this only after you've done the work of understanding what the text was trying to communicate. This way, the sermon points are from the text. They're not your ideas.

These divisions go back to the central idea and reiterate the central purpose based on the sermon idea: *Christians are called to suffer for the sake of preserving and proclaiming the gospel.*

The divisions would come right from this text:

- We suffer by the power of God (2 Tim. 1:8)
- We suffer for the sake of the gospel (2 Tim. 1:9-10)

Why should we be willing to embrace this suffering? The power of God enables and empowers us to do it. And because the gospel is *so* precious, we're absolutely willing to suffer; and because others who have gone before us have suffered, God gave them the grace to endure.

Once you have completed these steps, writing the sermon is easy. Understanding a text, its context, the central idea of the text, and then universalizing that idea gets you to a sermon idea guided by the text. Writing your sermon will flow directly from the text. If your sermon has been derived directly from the text and your points are based on the central idea of the text, if you've done the work to grasp the central idea, then your sermon divisions and points come from the natural flow of the text.

Because I do this work, I generally preach without notes. Sometimes, I might take a skeleton outline or a quote with me. But usually, I'll just have my text; and it will be highlighted in different colors where the different breaks are. This way, all I need when I preach is the text. It's my outline. My goal is to be faithful to the text. If you do the work, the same can be true for you.

✚

We've dealt with some technical details, and there's a lot more that could be said about those—but that is not the point. The point I want you to grasp is the connection between the art and the science of preaching, the commitment we must have to the text, and the discipline we can develop to get us into the text. This discipline also gets us into the text in such a way that we're looking at God and His message first through that human author to us and our audience. This changes the way we engage with the text. It changes the way we structure our sermons. It changes the way we think about what we're delivering to our people. It changes the entire purpose we're going after when preaching.

When people sit under this kind of preaching, they tend to get to a place of doxology. Even if it's a tough topic—like talking about suffering here—because the message is biblical, Christ-centered, and hope-filled, people come away feeling this doxological energy. God be praised for the grace He gives us to be able to endure! That's what happens when we look at the Scriptures and preaching and when we deliver it this way.

There's an illustration from my childhood that might help you remember this, regardless of where you are in your technical skills. When I was a kid, there was a pool in my neighborhood in Los Angeles. They had a swim team, and you could try out to be on that team. And so I did. I made the team. I was doing the best I could swimming freestyle. But even just doing freestyle, I was getting killed.

Next, they introduced the breaststroke and backstroke, and I could barely get across the pool. After that, they introduced the butterfly. For the life of me, I couldn't figure out how to do it. I just couldn't. I could still swim. But there were kids who could do all those strokes. They could do individual medley—freestyle, breaststroke, backstroke, and butterfly. They could do all those strokes and do them incredibly well, while I could barely make it across the pool.

I didn't last long being on the swim team, and I certainly never became an Olympic swimmer. But at the end of the day, I could still swim. I could still enjoy myself in the pool. I didn't have to give up on swimming. There were other sports that I did and at which I excelled.

These tools I've given you are just like those major strokes in the pool. Just because you're not doing them at the level of an Olympic swimmer doesn't mean you can't swim. If you swim enough, you'll get better. And you'll get faster. If you commit yourself to the art and science of preaching—if you commit yourself to prepare all your teaching this way—a year from now, you may not yet be a world-class theologian who is doing their work in the original languages. But you'll be a year better at doing these basic things than you are right now. You'll be a year better at digging out the marrow and the meaning of the text and communicating it to those who hear you.

And what about ten years from now? What about fifty years from now, should the Lord tarry and give you strength? If you keep this up, you may be an individual other people look at as an Olympic swimmer of preaching. For now, though, just take these basic tools, dig into the word, and be faithful to communicate the truth to whomever God places before you.

Chapter 7
Preaching and Prayer

Tim Dilena

Prayer is the lifeblood of a vital ministry with God,
yet many church leaders struggle with prayer.
Jesus left a precedent for prayer that we cannot—and should not—disregard.

"Prayer will singly assist you in the delivery of your sermon," C. H. Spurgeon said. "In fact, nothing so gloriously can fit you to preaching as descending fresh from the Mount of Communion so God can speak through you to men."[1] I want to show you this quote in action. I want to show you how Jesus descended from such a mountain of prayer and how ministry flowed.

We'll look at this from Luke 6:12-19:

> In these days he went out to the mountain to pray, and all night he continued in prayer to God. And when day came, he called his disciples and chose from them twelve, whom he named apostles: Simon, whom he named Peter, and Andrew his brother, and James and John, and Philip, and Bartholomew, and Matthew, and Thomas, and James the son of Alphaeus, and Simon who was called the Zealot, and Judas the son of James, and Judas

---

1   Charles Haddon Spurgeon, *Lectures to My Students* (Carol Stream: Tyndale House Publishers, 2010).

Iscariot, who became a traitor. And he came down with them and stood on a level place, with a great crowd of his disciples and a great multitude of people from all Judea and Jerusalem and the seacoast of Tyre and Sidon, who came to hear him and to be healed of their diseases. And those who were troubled with unclean spirits were cured. And all the crowd sought to touch him, for power came out from him and healed them all.

Henri Nouwen points out what he calls "three movements" in this passage, and he states that the order is important. These are solitude, community, and ministry.[2] In my upbringing, we would go right from solitude to ministry. But these days, the latest statistics show that most pastors pray less than four minutes a day. This means that many are essentially going from community to ministry and missing solitude altogether. All three of these components— which we could also refer to as devotional time, discipleship, and preaching— are important for effective ministry.

In Luke 6, Jesus spends an entire night in prayer and comes down from the mountain of prayer to His community, the twelve disciples. Only from there does Jesus move to a time of ministry. To skip any one of these renders preaching ineffective.

Solitude

Discipleship and preaching *must* be grounded in devotional time. Solitude is what makes community and ministry effective. Solitude is what causes you to have something to invest in others. But where there is no communion with God, there is no living Word. We have nothing to pour out. And when we have nothing to pour out, we try to find something from somebody else. We find ourselves plagiarizing.

From solitude flows community—investing deeply in the lives of a small group. It doesn't simply lead to ministry. That is the model of Jesus. Solitude

---

2   Henri J. M. Nouwen, *Reaching Out: The Three Movements of Spiritual Life* (Chadstone: Image Publishing, 1986).

before community is important because solitude helps us not to think of ourselves more highly than we ought. It's in solitude that we become naked before God; our hearts are open before God. As we look into the mirror of God's Word and into the face of God, God speaks to us.

Solitude helps us not to expect people to meet needs only God can meet. If we skip solitude and go right to community, we will put "God expectations" on people, expecting them to "be God" for us—all because we haven't communed with God and experienced the living God. Because we haven't gotten what we needed from God Himself, we put those expectations upon people—spouses, loved ones, friends, even pastors. We expect them to meet areas of our lives that only God can fulfill. And then we are disappointed when they don't meet those needs. But when we've been with God, we won't be asking people to be and do things for us that only God can be and do.

Community

Community—discipleship—is *not* about pouring into a church congregation. For Jesus, it was an investment into the twelve. For you, it could be pouring into your staff or discipling a small group of high-capacity leaders. It is more than simply hanging out with people, though. It's about pouring into people. But again, we cannot be effective in discipleship unless we experience God in solitude first. In solitude, we experience God's forgiveness, mercy, acceptance, and unmerited favor. This allows us to pour out to others what we've received from God.

But community is messy. In community, in dealing closely with a small group of people, there will be problems. Consider the challenges Jesus had with the twelve. There was Judas, the betrayer. And there was Simon Peter, later just known as Peter, a loose cannon. But two other disciples also stand out.

The first is someone we would probably, in today's vernacular, call a terrorist. In Jewish society, there were the Pharisees, the teachers. There were the Sadducees, experts in the law. There were the Essenes, who lived in seclusion. And there were the Zealots, the activists. The Zealots advocated taking back rule from Rome. They incited rebellion against Rome and despised those who represented Rome.

One of the twelve was Simon the Zealot. And then Jesus comes and puts Matthew, a tax collector, on the team. Jesus chose two people who were diametrically opposed to be among his small group of disciples. We don't read in the Bible all that went on between Simon and Matthew. I believe it's because of the time Jesus spent in solitude that He could model to them how to live with mercy, unmerited favor, unconditional love, and forgiveness.

In community, we will likewise face those types of relationships that need revelation from God for how to deal with challenging individuals in whom we are investing. That is why solitude *must* come before community. In solitude, we will experience God's mercy, favor, love, and forgiveness firsthand. This way, we will have something to pass on. Once we embrace solitude, then forgiveness in this community becomes easy. Forgiveness becomes the cement of community. And we can model and teach forgiveness because we've experienced forgiveness. We've experienced unconditional love from God the Father.

The danger of jumping from solitude to ministry is that we make church about personality instead of legacy. Ministry becomes about stage presence. We can become transfixed on praying and getting a word from Heaven in order to jump ahead to preach, create a podcast, or post a sermon online, so we can see how many views we get. But in community, we are involved in the lives of people, preparing them for ministry for decades to come. It's not just about being in their ears on a Sunday.

D. L. Moody, the great American evangelist, said, "I'd rather be a great *pray*er than a great preacher. Jesus never taught his disciples how to preach. He only taught them how to pray."[3] I believe that is what

---

3   D. L. Moody, "Anecdotes, Incidents, and Illustrations (sermon, 1898).

Jesus was doing in solitude and community. The challenge is for us to be consistent in our time of solitude first, then be effective in discipleship so we can move into effective ministry. And we must do this despite the vast demands upon our time. Carving out consistent time to read the Bible typically isn't the issue. The challenge is getting to our knees. And if we don't fight to get a consistent time of solitude and prayer, we'll easily skip it.

Be Consistent in Prayer

Our time of solitude is about more than simply praying and reading the Bible to get a sermon. It's about knowing God. How, then, do we become consistent in our time of solitude and get to know God?

I have five quotes that I keep in my prayer journal and read before I spend time in prayer. The first is from David Wilkerson, who often said, "God always makes a way for a praying man."[4] The next is from Walter Wink, who said, "History belongs to the intercessors."[5] The third quote is from Martin Luther, who said, "He who has prayed well has studied well." I've seen the difference between a well-studied sermon and a well-prayed-over sermon. The difference between those two is authority. The next quote is from the great Scottish preacher, Samuel Chadwick. He said, "Hurry is the death of prayer." And finally, I have a quote from Leonard Ravenhill, a great writer of revival, who said, "To be much for God, we must be much with God."[6]

Before you spend time in solitude, tell God this in prayer: *Lord God, I want to be consistent in prayer. God, it is true that You always make a way for a praying*

---

4   David Wilkerson, "Seeking God in the Secret Place," World Challenge, January 22, 2016, https://www.worldchallenge.org/seeking-god-secret-place.

5   Walter Wink, "History Belongs to the Intercessors," Amazon Web Services, Accessed September 2, 2024, https://celectcdn.s3.amazonaws.com/files/0024/6892/2012.01.08. pastors_blog.pdf.

6   Leonard Ravenhill, "Praying, Sinning, Your Only Hope for Revival," The Majesty's Men, Accessed September 2, 2024, https://themajestysmen.com/quotes/leonard-ravenhill-praying-sinning-quote.

man, that history belongs to the intercessors, that he who has prayed well has studied well, and that hurry is the death of prayer. God, I know that to be much for You; I must be much with you.

Then, be with Jesus. It would be wrong for me just to simply tell you, "You need to pray more." But when I was nineteen, starting my first job as a pastor, I discovered a verse that became my model for consistency in prayer: "And rising very early in the morning, while it was still dark, he departed and went out to a desolate place, and there he prayed" (Mark 1:35). This verse provides us with four practical lessons from Jesus's prayer life. It has brought consistency for me in terms of the area of solitude.

1. WHEN: Find the Time with the Fewest Distractions and Put It on Your Calendar.

Jesus went to pray in the early morning. Define the time with the fewest disruptions for you. When our son was an infant, he would get up early in the morning. I would get up, give him a bottle, turn on a kid's television show, put on headphones, and pray. He would lean against my back while I prayed. We made it work. I found time to pray.

Nowadays, our four kids are teenagers, and teens don't get up early. When I get up early in the morning, the house is quiet. Also, nobody texts me early in the morning. But your time doesn't have to be in the morning. Just find the time with the fewest disruptions. When our children were young, I would pray at night after putting our daughter Anna in her crib. For her to fall asleep, I had to hold her hand. I could do that while I was on the floor praying. It worked. No one was coming into the baby's room. They knew I was putting Anna to sleep and praying.

Whatever time you choose, put it on your schedule. If *you* don't schedule your time, people will schedule your time for you. Sometimes, people ask to meet with me in the morning. I don't do that. I don't grab coffee with people, even early in the morning. When people ask me to have morning meetings or calls, I simply tell them, "I already have an appointment. I'm sorry I can't meet with you." My mornings are blocked off for time with God.

Sometimes, when people realize I don't have any mornings free, they might ask, "Who are you meeting with every morning?" That's when I would share that my meeting is with God. If anybody were to be offended, I would tell them that they really need me to meet with God in order to talk to them. If I don't talk with God, I can't invest in community, else I would put God expectations upon people.

2. HOW: Get Up!

Jesus got physically ready. He got up. For me, getting up to pray was a game-changer. I don't do well lying in bed praying, not even sitting in bed praying. I must get up and get out of bed. I cannot lay on the ground praying, either, or else that turns into another hour of sleep. If I want to create consistency in praying, I must put myself in a position where I won't fall back asleep.

3. WHERE: Have a Place Where You Meet Jesus Every Day.

Jesus went to a secluded place. He had a place where he would go to be alone in prayer.

For consistency, there must be a place that you always go to, a place where you meet Jesus. One of the blessings I have here at Times Square Church is that I pray with the elders on the phone from six to seven every single morning. I go to a room and close the door so I won't wake up my wife or my family, and I pray with the elders. For you, it may be finding a spot in your living room, one chair where you go and pray. Or perhaps you always go for a prayer walk in your neighborhood. Pick a place where you consistently spend time praying.

4. WHAT: Simply Pray.

According to Mark 1:35, Jesus simply prayed. He didn't text. He didn't listen to music. He didn't read his Bible, the Torah. Jesus prayed.

I come from a Pentecostal background, so I was taught to pray in the Spirit and sometimes forgot how to simply pray in English. One thing that has helped me to build a new vocabulary for prayer is to pray using God's Word. As you go through the New Testament, pay attention to Paul's prayers—often at the start or end of his letters—then use those as a model for praying. These prayers help my mind not to wander because I'm paying attention to what I am reading and praying. Other times, I pray the Psalms. As I'm speaking God's Word, it engages my mind and my mouth.

I love what Thomas Keating says about prayer: "The only way to fail in prayer is to not show up."[7] That's why the enemy wants us to be inconsistent.

Learn to Hear God's Heartbeat

When I first started in ministry, I didn't understand the importance of being consistent in prayer and solitude. I was missing what God was wanting to do through daily times of solitude. As a result, the two worst days of my week were Saturdays and Mondays. On Saturdays, I'd be begging God for a word for Sunday. And on Mondays, I'd be judging myself for how poorly I had done. And then I had to do it all over again. It was maddening.

There's a familiar story in the gospel of John that helped open my eyes. It became the cement for me in going from solitude to community and over into ministry. In John 13:21-26, we find this encounter between Jesus and the twelve. They are at the Last Supper; and in this passage, there are three main characters: Jesus, Peter, and John, who refers to himself as the disciple whom Jesus loved.

> "Truly, truly, I say to you, one of you will betray me." The disciples looked at one another, uncertain of whom he spoke.

---

7   Thomas Keating, *Open Mind, Open Heart* (New York: Continuum Press, 2006).

> One of his disciples, whom Jesus loved, was reclining at table
> at Jesus' side, so Simon Peter motioned to him to ask Jesus of
> whom he was speaking. So that disciple, leaning back against
> Jesus, said to him, "Lord, who is it?" Jesus answered, "It is he to
> whom I will give this morsel of bread when I have dipped it."
> So when he had dipped the morsel, he gave it to Judas, the son
> of Simon Iscariot.

Look at it again. Jesus says that one of the twelve was going to betray Jesus. I'm sure every one of them had to have wondered, *Is it me? Will I betray Jesus?* Peter was always asking questions, and that's what he does here again. But instead of asking Jesus, Peter asks John, who is leaning against Jesus's chest, to ask Jesus who will do it. Then Jesus addresses John, saying, "It is he to whom I will give this morsel of bread when I have dipped it." Jesus was telling John that Judas would be the betrayer.

Do you understand what just happened here? Peter is just one person over from Jesus; but instead of asking Jesus, Peter asks John (him) what Jesus means instead of asking Jesus (Him).

When you make solitude a priority, you discover the difference between "the big *H*" and "the little *h*." Therein lies the secret of sermon preparation.

The secret of preaching with authority, of breaking free from Monday morning depression, is to be so close to Jesus that we are leaning against Jesus's bosom and hearing the heartbeat of God. Peter, like most of us, asked John—the one leaning against Jesus's bosom—what Jesus is saying instead of leaning in and talking to Jesus and hearing what Jesus has to say. I spent most of my life asking others what God says, and I'm finally learning to lean in and listen directly to what God says. Many of us lean on the "leaners" instead of becoming leaners ourselves and hearing God's heart for the people we minister to week after week.

If you want to deliver God's heart to your people, don't rely on someone else to tell you what God is saying to *them*. Lean in. Get close to Jesus so you can hear His heartbeat. Getting *that* close takes time, though. It takes discipline. That's why what Luther said is poignant: "He who has prayed well has studied well." In solitude and prayer, we hear the heart of Jesus.

I'm not encouraging you not to be well-studied. I'm pleading with you to become someone who leans against God's chest. I'm pleading with you to come to the big *H* instead of asking the little *h* what God says. A little *h* could be everything from a podcast to listening to another sermon on YouTube. It could be leaning on a commentary or a book or input from a mentor. I'm not saying that what those sources are saying isn't from the heart of Jesus. What I *am* saying is that you can lean in and ask Jesus first. It's a matter of placement and priority. The priority is that the big *H* comes before the little *h*.

It's a matter of at what point do we turn to those commentaries, podcasts, books, and sound teaching by other pastors? They may be legit, but they cannot come first. Leaning in and resting your head on God's chest is the priority, so you can hear God's heartbeat for your city and your community.

At a roundtable some years ago, someone asked a pastor friend of mine, "What is God saying to the Church?"

I loved my friend's answer. He said, "Is God saying something to the Church? I don't think he's saying something to the Church. I think he's saying ten thousand things to the Church. When you read the book of Revelation, Jesus is not saying the same thing to Ephesus as He is to Laodicea as he is to Smyrna. He spoke definitively and specifically to each church. As a pastor, you must find out what God is saying to *your* church."

It was like Peter asking John to know what Jesus has to say. My friend pointed back to the big *H*. We can learn to lean our heads on God's chest through solitude and through finding consistency in being in the presence of God. I've listened to well-studied preachers and well-prayed-up preachers. The former—those who start with the little *h*—can craft a masterpiece of a sermon with every point alliterating. I'm not saying alliteration is wrong. I'm not saying using illustrations is wrong either. But there's something about the preacher who hears Jesus's heartbeat *first*. So start preparation with the big *H*.

Practically speaking, what does that look like? Whatever passage or topic you'll be preaching on, before you even open a commentary, before you listen to a podcast or listen to a sermon on the topic, take your Bible, take your notebook, lay on the floor, and listen for God's heartbeat. Find the place that John occupied. There's room enough for you to be there. Jesus wants you to place your ear against His chest to hear what saddens His heart and what makes it glad. You can only do that in solitude and prayer.

Do I still turn to my library during sermon preparation? Of course! It's just that I have it in the right priority.[8] I've tried all my life to read a book a week. But for me, it has become a priority to start with the big *H* first, asking Jesus what His heart is about an issue before I turn to my library.

✝

During a visit to Boston, I took a photo that I've saved as the lock screen on my iPad. I usually preach using my iPad, so I see this picture every time before I preach. It's of a statue of the great American preacher Phillips Brooks. Brooks is preaching with one hand on the Bible, and the other hand is up in the air. Behind him stands Jesus with His hand on Brooks' shoulder.

This picture reminds me that I want to experience this every time I preach. I want to communicate God's heart to whomever I have the honor of speaking. And I want to feel Jesus' hand upon me. To do that, I must hear the heart of the big *H* first before turning to the little *h*.

---

8   One of my favorite sermons on the placement of books is Spurgeon's sermon on 2 Timothy 4:13. Spurgeon's message is called, "Paul—His Cloak and His Books." Spurgeon shows the proper placement of books and the Scriptures.

Chapter 8
Preaching with Passion

Claude Houde

Preaching with a true consuming passion does not come from personality, charisma,
temperament, or age. It comes from utter submission to God. Such divinely gifted
fervor in your preaching will result in fruit within your congregation.

Ministering to leaders, pastors, communicators, or preachers has
exponential potential for the kingdom of God. That is why God said to
Moses, "I will take my Spirit and place it upon you, Moses. And I will put
that same Spirit upon the elders and the entire congregation."[1] In other
words, if you touch and minister and give life to leaders, the whole body of
Christ will benefit. This is so close to my heart and an invitation I do not
take for granted.

I've been preaching for almost forty years. I've preached all over the
world at churches, outreach events, and pastors' conferences with tens of
thousands of leaders in attendance. At one such conference, I was with Pastor
Gary Wilkerson in Kinshasa in the Democratic Republic of the Congo. At that
event, there were ten thousand pastors; and hearing such a crowd praying in
unison to me was the sound of Heaven. Someone snapped a picture of me

---

1   Numbers 11:17, 25

sitting and reading my Bible just before I addressed those pastors. I didn't know they were taking it. To me, that picture represents preaching with passion—just the man and his Bible and God, a man in communion with the Holy Spirit to deliver the Word of the Lord.

Preaching with passion is not a matter of the size of the crowd, though. In my early years of ministry, I used to preach in small churches all over the French world and in the nation of Québec. There would be fifty, thirty, twenty people—just a pastor and a few people, but we were blessed with the same passion. Passion is a matter of communion with God. Communion with God gives us the conviction and courage to communicate with supernatural capacity, preach with passion, and advance the kingdom of God. Preaching with passion will bring fire and fervor; but more than that, it will bear fruit.

After decades of ministry, I am blessed to testify that from a couple of dozen people at the beginning, *Nouvelle Vie* (New Life Church) has grown to over five thousand people today. I am also honored to lead a movement of churches throughout the francophone world, along with a mercy agency that serves and feeds over fifteen thousand people every month. And I am the president of the board of an accredited Bible college that trains people for the ministry with a bachelor's and master's program. We have over a thousand graduates ministering throughout the French world.

I say this to underscore the fact that preaching with passion will bear fruit. Preaching with passion is theology with testimonies. It's ministry that allows us to enter into the miraculous. It's truth that transcends time and tradition. Preaching with passion is triumph with tears. It is also inward terror. It never gets easy to bring an infusion of transformation.

Preaching with passion is never for our glory, and it's never guaranteed. It's not received once and for all. It needs to be renewed over and over. Preaching with passion is inspiration for incarnation and illumination, and it initiates a supernatural impact that brings us into the realm of the impossible.

Preaching with passion is announcing, pronouncing, and denouncing. It is comforting the afflicted, and it's afflicting the comfortable.

Three Dynamics of Preaching with Passion

A passionate Preacher Himself, God gives us an introductory picture of preaching with passion in many places in the Scriptures. Here, we'll look at four foundational truths from the book of Malachi.

> My covenant with him was one of life and peace, and I gave them to him. It was a covenant of fear, and he feared me. He stood in awe of my name. True instruction was in his mouth, and no wrong was found on his lips. He walked with me in peace and uprightness, and he turned many from iniquity. For the lips of a priest should guard knowledge, and people should seek instruction from his mouth, for he is the messenger of the LORD of hosts (Mal. 2:5-7).

Based upon this passage, the first dynamic of preaching with passion is confidence and covenant. "My covenant with him was one of life and peace," Malachi says. Every time we speak or teach, no matter what the circumstances are, how strong or weak we may feel, what the size of the congregation is, what our emotions are, or whether we are preaching in person or delivering an online message to a camera in an empty sanctuary, we are in covenant with God.

We must stand with confidence in this covenant. We must speak with confidence no matter how weak, feeble or inadequate, or overwhelmed we may feel. We are God's mouthpiece. We are speaking His name, kingdom, purposes, and Divine will. When we're preaching with passion, there's a dynamic of confidence and covenant.

There's also a dynamic of conscience and conduct. In Malachi 2, God is basically saying, "I gave My commands, Divine principle, and laws to my servant, my communicator, so he might fear Me, be reverent before My name, and tremble before Me." That is an essential question we must ask ourselves. After all these years of preaching, do I still stand in reverence and tremble at the awesome responsibility of bringing the Word of God to people, knowing full well, as James teaches, that those who teach God's people will be judged more severely?[2] We're not only responsible for our lives but also for what we preach. There's a dynamic of having confidence in His covenant and my conscience regarding my conduct.

There's also a principle of confrontation and courage. "True instruction was in his mouth, and no wrong was found on his lips. He walked with me in peace and uprightness, and he turned many from iniquity" (Mal. 2:6). We're not stand-up comics. We're not political pundits. We're not just theological orators. We're not happy gurus. We are messengers of God preaching with passion.

We have a sense of confronting the culture in this twenty-first century, confronting it with courage. The law of God is on our lips, and many come to us. There's no deceit. There's a sense of confidence and covenant, a sense of conscience and conduct, and there's a sense of confrontation and courage so that many will turn away from their sin.

Finally, there's the dynamic of continuity in calling. "For the lips of a priest should guard knowledge, and people should seek instruction from his mouth, for he is the messenger of the Lord of hosts" (Mal. 2:7). Passion is not in personality. It's not in charisma. It's not a temperament. It's not it's in human emotion. It's not a matter of culture. And it's not a matter of age. It's a matter of heart and standing in communion with God.

Three Characteristics of Preaching with Passion

Allow me to share a vignette from standing next to one of the most passionate preachers I've been privileged to walk with and minister

2   James 3:1

with—Pastor David Wilkerson, the founder of World Challenge. In 1985, he came to minister in the nation of Québec in response to a calling from God. I was his interpreter from English into French. He came to our nation; and for five weeks, I traveled with him.

Now, spiritual passion is not a matter of what you have achieved in the past or how much experience you may have at this point. I was just in my twenties, and Brother Dave was in his fifties. He was world-renowned; but here he was, ministering to much smaller crowds in Québec than what he was used to. We had a conference for pastors where he ministered for four sessions. That evening, we went to a hockey arena, where he preached an amazing message and stayed a long time praying with hundreds who had given their lives to Christ. Afterward, there was a news conference and media interviews, and it all went on late into the night. It was long after midnight by the time we got back to the hotel, and we had to leave very early the next day.

Of course, this was before we had the internet and cell phones. I got a call from the front desk at three in the morning. There had been an emergency in Texas, and I was asked to go wake up Mr. Wilkerson for a phone call.

As I approached his room, I heard what I thought was a baby or a woman sobbing. I double-checked that I was at the right room and, very timidly, knocked. Brother Dave opened the door, tears running down his face.

"Sir, I'm sorry," I told him, "but there's a call for you downstairs."

I went downstairs with him to take the call; but before we came back upstairs, we just sat for a while, both wide awake in the middle of the night. So, I asked him, "You weren't sleeping, sir?"

He hesitated, but then he told me, "No. I don't like to talk about this; but the Lord has shown me on evangelistic nights—when the gospel is preached and so many come to Christ—that the enemy goes to steal the seed from the hearts, even in the hours after the message. The Lord has called me to pray for Him to protect the seed, to protect the work that He had done."

I remember going to bed that night and lying there thinking, *Here I am sleeping. And there's this man of God who has a worldwide ministry, and he's weeping for my people!*

This was three decades ago; and I still meet pastors, leaders, and people who were saved in those services. Passion in preaching is not a matter of age; it's about a heart that is connected to God's passion. It is a communication of God's passion to us. I would like to suggest three main characteristics of preaching with passion.

1. Passionate Preaching Is Life-Giving.

In 2 Corinthians 3:6, we read, "Who has made us sufficient to be ministers of a new covenant, not of the letter but of the Spirit. For the letter kills, but the Spirit gives life." This is God's standard for an adequate, accepted, and sufficient ministry of preaching. Once He has made us sufficient as ministers, our message must be life-giving. It must give supernatural life. It must lead to eternal life. It must give life to what was dead in people. It must give life to families and to couples. It must give life so that we can love, forgive, and rebuild.

It brings forth results. Paul shows us very specific manifestations of this life-giving, passionate preaching. He teaches that life-giving preaching brings forth results. "Are we beginning to commend ourselves again? Or do we need, as some do, letters of recommendation to you, or from you? You yourselves are our letter of recommendation, written on our hearts, to be known and read by all. And you show that you are a letter from Christ delivered by us, written not with ink but with the Spirit of the living God, not on tablets of stone but on tablets of human hearts" (2 Cor. 3:1-3).

The apostle Paul says passionate preaching is not of the letter, for the letter kills. But it is of the Spirit, for the Spirit gives life. Such preaching brings forth results. That's the standard. That is proof of the legitimacy of our ministry. That is proof of its authenticity.

The confirmation of our ministry is not in letters and diplomas. It's not in titles. It's not in denominational posturing or positioning. It's not in seniority, experience, or expertise. The fruit that life-giving preaching brings forth is in the lives that are changed, in those who are living epistles read by all men. Passionate, life-giving preaching seeks an Emmaus Road experience. Every time we speak for God, people's hearts will burn within them as we expound on the Word of God. Life-giving preaching brings forth conversions. People get saved. People turn from their sins. People repent. Their spiritual eyes are opened as scales fall from their eyes. Life-giving preaching leads to people forgiving each other. People become generous. People are entering the kingdom of God.

It comes from revelation. Life-giving, passionate preaching is the result of revelation. Paul says in 2 Corinthians 3:4-6, "Such is the confidence that we have through Christ toward God. Not that we are sufficient in ourselves to claim anything as coming from us, but our sufficiency is from God, who has made us sufficient to be ministers of a new covenant." We are not capable of bringing forth life by ourselves. We study, and we pray. We prepare. But those are only loaves and fishes that we bring to God. In and of ourselves, we cannot conceive anything eternal. It is in our communion with God that we receive revelation. Our confidence must be in God and our sufficiency from God. Life-giving, passionate preaching is to hear the call of God; and in hearing, we become a voice, not an echo.

In this generation where preachers are listening online to so many things, we can grab at what others are saying. Yes, there is a place for studying and for being inspired. But life-giving preaching comes by revelation. It reflects God's glory. Paul says in the same chapter, "And we all, with unveiled face, beholding the glory of the Lord, are being transformed into the same image from one degree of glory to another. For this comes from the Lord who is the Spirit" (2 Cor. 3:18). Life-giving preaching takes place as we are being transformed to bring transformation to others. Here are some good questions to ask on our knees:

- *Lord, am I running on old sermon ideas from years past? Or am I running on my own energy?*
- *Am I allowing You to transform me so I am not only a reflection of my denomination, a reflection of my favorite preacher, or a reflection of the times?*
- *Am I allowing You to transform me to transform others?*
- *Am I reflecting Your love, justice, holiness, and awesomeness in my preaching?*
- *Am I reflecting Your patience, character, passion, accessibility, and authority?*

2. Passionate Preaching Is Preaching with Spiritual Authority.

To preach with passion is to preach with spiritual authority. Matthew says it this way: "And when Jesus finished these sayings, the crowds were astonished at his teaching, for he was teaching them as one who had authority, and not as their scribes" (Matt. 7:28-29). The scribes could expound on the law all day long. But Jesus spoke with authority.

It's not about volume. Preaching with spiritual authority lies not in the volume or the tone of our voices. It's not about screaming. We can scream until we're blue in the face and not have a trace of spiritual authority. It's also not about intimidation. The easiest and most deceiving part of training in boxing is the part when you shadowbox. You can get to a place where you think highly of yourself. But shadowboxing is just a lot of movement with no impact, adversary, opponent, nor hitting back. Passionate preaching is not spiritual shadowboxing. Meanwhile, preaching *without* spiritual authority is a lot of movement and a lot of yelling without actual spiritual impact.

It's not about age. Speaking to a young Timothy who was intimidated by older men around him, Paul said, "For God gave us a spirit not of fear but of power and love and self-control" (2 Tim. 1:7). Preaching with spiritual authority is not a matter of age. The same is true for experienced ministers. Preaching with spiritual authority is not a guarantee. It's not something you acquire once and for all. Your experience does not give you spiritual authority.

In his latter years, Solomon completely lost that authority.[3] Eli the high priest also lost all discernment and authority in his later years.[4] And in his latter years, even Samson did not know that the hand of God had been removed from him.[5]

It's not about personality. Decades of ministry and preaching have proved to me what I refer to as the absolute limitations of human or natural authority. Personality does not help you when you are facing spiritual battles. Remember, Paul said, "We do not wrestle against flesh and blood, but against the rulers, against the authorities, against the cosmic powers over this present darkness, against the spiritual forces of evil in the heavenly places" (Eph. 6:12). When we bring out the Word of God, there is something spiritual going on, and personality won't help us stand against those forces of darkness. Instead, we need to preach spiritual authority.

It's not about knowledge. Hosea says, "My people are destroyed for lack of knowledge" (Hosea 4:6). Spiritual authority, though, is not proportionate to knowledge or academic credentials. I've dedicated a large portion of my life and ministry to theological training. I believe in solid theological training. But plenty of perfectly sound, educated theologians are without any spiritual authority over sin or evil, the lies and snares of the enemy, the demonic, and addictions or deceit. They have no authority to reverse shame, guilt, blindness, and despair. Academics only can give us respect and acclaim but not spiritual authority.

---

3   1 Kings 11:4-11
4   1 Samuel 4:13-18
5   Judges 16

It's not about credentials. Spiritual authority also does not lie in our accreditation. I lead a movement with hundreds of credential-holders. We have academic, moral, and ministerial standards. I believe in standards and credentials, but those don't give us spiritual authority. In all my years of ministry, demons never asked for my credentials. Even in me standing against deception, depression, despair, doubt, and diseases, the devil never asked for my credentials.

It's not automatic. Men and women with ten, twenty, or thirty years of ministry: your authority today is not automatic because you had seasons—or maybe decades—of spiritual authority in your life. Spiritual authority is also not automatically renewed or transferred due to decades of preaching ministry. Saul's armor had been in many battles, but it became utterly useless when facing new giants.[6] It had no authority. As for Elijah, he was terrified of Jezebel's threats, even asking to die.[7] Meanwhile, shortly before, he had stood in supernatural authority against the prophets of Baal, seeing fire fall from Heaven.[8] There are way too many modern-day tragedies and moral failures in the pulpit that bring shame and reproach to all of us, events that erase years and years of serving God. So I am daily reminded that you and I cannot rely or rest on yesterday's spiritual authority in our life and ministry. We must seek it afresh today.

It's not the same as spiritual abuse. Spiritual authority is not about manipulation. It's not about domination, nepotism, or self-preservation. It's not about gaining control through preaching. Instead, spiritual authority is the power and Divine authority through communion with the Holy Spirit for continued communication that will produce supernatural conviction, conversion, consecration, compassion, correction, change, conquest, and eternal crowns. If passionate preaching means we preach with such spiritual authority, then we must seek that authority passionately

---

6   1 Samuel 17:38-39
7   1 Kings 19:1-4
8   1 Kings 18:25-46

through communion with the Holy Spirit. In doing so, God's authority can be communicated to us and through us for this season of our lives. This will produce the authority to reverse darkness and blindness. It will produce supernatural conviction, conversion, consecration, compassion, and correction. People will change because this spiritual authority brings spiritual conquest. It brings spiritual crowns.

3. Passionate Preaching Is Preaching with Urgency

The apostle Paul, in his letter to the church in Corinth, said:

> For we must all appear before the judgment seat of Christ, so that each one may receive what is due for what he has done in the body, whether good or evil. Therefore, knowing the fear of the Lord, we persuade others. But what we are is known to God, and I hope it is known also to your conscience. . . For if we are beside ourselves, it is for God; if we are in our right mind, it is for you. For the love of Christ controls us. . . Therefore, we are ambassadors for Christ, God making his appeal through us. We implore you on behalf of Christ, be reconciled to God. (2 Cor. 5:10-11, 13-14, 20).

Preaching with passion is preaching with urgency because we will all appear before the judgment seat of God. We know the terror of men and women slipping into eternity without God. Are we preparing every message with such a sense of responsibility?

In the very beginning years of our church, we had some experiences that fashioned and deepened my sense of urgency in preaching. I remember this one young girl who had been badly abused in her childhood, which led to several challenges. This girl ended up being a victim of school bullying in the worst way, and she began to entertain thoughts of suicide.

One Saturday night, when this girl was a teenager, she took all the pills she could get her hands on. Doctors later said she should have died. But she had a friend, a young lady from our church who had been witnessing to her and inviting her to come to church. After taking the pills, the girl was lying there, feeling the drugs taking over. And in the midst of it all, she saw the face of her friend saying, "Go to the church." In a zombie state, she made her way to the church and sat in a chair. An usher saw her and called the ambulance, and she was rushed to the hospital. They saved her life.

Québec had some of the highest rates of suicide in the world at the time, so some of the leaders at our church and I would frequently walk through the sanctuary, laying hands on the chairs and praying. We still do it. We do it with a sense that for whoever will come and sit in those chairs, it's a matter of life and death.

As for the young woman, after she was released from the hospital, she began coming to church. The suicidal ideation stopped. She met a young man she married. She's now a mother in our church.

There must be an urgency to our passion. Week after week, we must seek to persuade men and women of the gospel. The apostle Paul described it as being "beside ourselves." The Corinthians were getting sophisticated; they were probably getting a bit embarrassed at Paul's passion, so he reminded them, "If I seem beside myself to you, it is because of God. It is because the love of God controls me."[9]

What compels you in your preaching? I ask this with no finger-pointing, no condemnation. It is easy to be compelled and motivated and driven by numbers, fame, approval, money, or likes and follows on social media. It is easy to be compelled by developing a ministry and ministerial reputation. It could be the love of being accepted by this society. But old-fashioned, passionate preaching says, "We are ambassadors for God. The love of God poured out in our hearts by the Holy Spirit compels us to beg you to be reconciled with God." That love of God takes us to a place where we cry out to God, "Lord, I need a word from you!"

---

9   2 Corinthians 5:14

✛

When I think of a spiritual passion that is life-giving, has spiritual authority, and is delivered with urgency, I think of a moment Brother David Wilkerson and I had in France. We had been teaching at pastoral conferences throughout the country; and they ran us ragged, non-stop, day after day. But this one Friday, we had the day free before a big evangelistic rally that night and another packed Saturday and Sunday. We had our wives with us, and the ladies wanted to go see some of the beautiful areas along the Mediterranean Coast, so we went someplace gorgeous for brunch that Friday.

But as time went on, I could sense Brother Dave getting more and more preoccupied. "I'm sorry," he told us. "I've got to go prepare."

We were having an evangelistic rally that night at a football stadium in Cannes, and the organizers were expecting as many as five thousand people. France is a very secular country; and in a crowd like what we would be facing, maybe a thousand would be Christians. He and I returned to the hotel; and as was the case, we met about an hour and a half before the service to go over his message so that I would be prepared to translate.

Everything seemed fine. But for the first time in all the years we had worked together, Brother Dave closed the notes and said, "That's not the word. I have no word."

I tried to assure him that what he had was a good message, but he said, "I've been praying, and this is not the word. I have no word."

Still, we got into the car and made our way through traffic to the soccer stadium.

At the arena, he asked to be taken to a room. All they had was a locker room, so that's where they took him; and we left him there. Meanwhile, the event was starting. A choir was singing; and the pastors were getting nervous, so they asked me to please go and get him.

When I opened the door, Brother Dave was lying face down on the cement floor, screaming, "I have no word! If you don't give me a word, I cannot go out. Lord, give me a word, please. Give me a word!"

We were minutes away from him speaking, but I just shut the door and prayed.

Soon after, he came out, tears all over his face, and he told to me, "I have a word."

You can imagine how relieved I was. We walked onto the stage, where I introduced him. The crowd was rowdy, though. They kept whistling and talking, just like they had throughout the choir singing. I was starting to get more agitated. Here was Brother Dave, a man in his seventies at the time. He looked feeble, like a grandfather. When I introduced him, I asked the crowd—most of them in their twenties—to please show some respect and welcome Evangelist David Wilkerson.

They didn't clap. They just kept talking. Still, Brother Dave got up and slowly walked to the podium. He put down his Bible and looked at the crowd. I stood there, ready to interpret. What happened next is hard to describe. When he began speaking, it was as if a cloud came down on that stadium. The crowd grew quiet, listening intently.

Brother Dave spoke only for twenty-five minutes or so, and then he did an altar call. But this was like an anti-altar call. He was saying things like, "If you are coming just because you're in trouble and you want to try God, stay in your place. If you want to keep your religion and keep your traditions and try Jesus, stay in your place. If you don't want to leave your sins, stay in your place."

Remember, France is a highly secular country. The organizers were expecting maybe a hundred people to come forward. But more than half of the people in the stadium came forward that night! They didn't know how this works; so the first ones walked right on stage, filling the stage and then the area in front of the stage. There were thousands of young people surrounding us, wanting to pray.

This was the case of a man standing in the authority of God, preaching with passion a life-giving word with urgency. His passionate preaching demonstrated the heart of God communicated to us and through us with spiritual authority and urgency. It was life-giving. We can never create this passion on our own.

Chapter 9
Preaching Biblical Repentance

John Bailey

We are called to preach in power. God's Word is necessary to have effective preaching. The presence of God through the Holy Spirit is essential to powerful preaching. Preaching repentance is foundational but many times is not emphasized. A culture of repentance will create soil that can receive the Word and produce eternal fruit.

In Matthew 4:16, Matthew refers to a quote from the time of Isaiah. Obviously, the darkness spoken of applies to the days Jesus lived. What cannot be missed is that this Scripture applies to all times and places throughout human history, including our own. From the time of the Fall until this day, humanity has had this undeniable bend to darkness. Glory to God that in the midst of a dark and broken world, Jesus shines brightly to all who believe. The second thing that cannot be missed is that Jesus, after being tempted in the desert following baptism, begins His public ministry. His first message Matthew records is a message of repentance! Repentance is a foundational aspect of all true biblical preaching.

Only a brief time after marrying the love of my life, Crista, I attempted to surprise her by cleaning the house while she was out shopping. As she walked through the doors, I was so proud of myself. "I cleaned the house!" Just a small window into my personality, I tend to be great with vision, even organization. However, paying attention to details, particularly in my cleaning skills, is lacking.

After looking around, she politely tried to protect my pride. "Thank you for straightening up the house . . . Let's take a little time, and I want to show you what clean is."

For the next few hours, my new bride pulled out the rubber gloves, all-purpose cleaner, window cleaner, buckets, mops, and scrub brushes; and I began to understand the difference between a surface clean and a "deep" clean. Here is the truth: in the Church, we spend too much of our energy doing surface cleaning when men and women need a deep clean. Over the next few pages, I want to dive into the Scriptures and underscore how it defines true biblical repentance.

The Perpetuity of the Gospel

Perpetuity is a fifteenth-century English word that helps us understand the power of the gospel and repentance. Perpetuity is defined by two concepts: eternal truth and long-term investment. The gospel and Jesus' words are unchanging. The kingdom message transcends all times and all people. Also, the gospel carries an element of producing long-term fruit in a changed life. A perpetual annuity is a picture of the gospel never changing in its essence while at the same time multiplying in its effect.

Here are some gospel truth passages about repentance:

- "Heaven and earth will pass away, but my words will not pass away" (Matt. 24:35).
- "Bear fruit in keeping with repentance" (Matt. 3:8).

Repentance Is Defined by Turning To and Away

C. S. Lewis said, "[Repentance] means unlearning all the self-conceit and self-will that we have been training ourselves into for thousands of years."[1] As a missionary for eight years traveling to many places on five continents, I have had many opportunities to experience diverse cultures. In observing cross-cultural communication, I have come to understand that cultures are a culmination of behavior over many generations. The values of a northern European can be far different from the values of someone who resides in central Africa or Southeast Asia.

There is no greater cultural renewal than when a man or woman comes to faith in Christ. Living in the kingdom of God is a complete change in values, lifestyles, and priorities that is distinct from every culture and people group in the world. We do not lose our God-given individuality in the process, but the change in our thinking and character will be an incredible shift. When we begin living in a Christ culture, our values are synchronized with His. What we live for changes. What we value changes. Our lifestyle should have a radical transformation. Salvation is free by God's grace completely. As Jesus says, we have been transferred from the kingdom of darkness to the kingdom of light!

Far too often in ministry, we are content to have many people attend our churches and drop some money in the basket. However, Jesus is most concerned with making disciples. The final command of Jesus is to go to the nations and make disciples.[2] The command is not to have a great following, sell books, build large buildings, or be respected in our communities. I'm thankful if these things happen, but the command is to make disciples—to preach and teach all that Christ has spoken, turning away from our sin and turning to Jesus.

---

1   Lewis, *Mere Christianity*.
2   Matthew 28:19

When church growth focuses on an unoffensive message and entertainment, we forfeit what is most powerful about the gospel. Biblical church growth is when believers are transformed by the gospel, turn to Christ, experience new birth, and are conformed to His character! This person will affect his or her community and the world in a powerful way. Western Christian culture is starving for biblical authenticity produced by living disciples. The path to discipleship is biblical repentance.

Unbiblical Repentance versus Biblical Repentance

I surrendered my life to Christ in jail almost forty years ago. The Lord did a powerful work in my life; and every day, I am thankful for His kindness. Not too long after coming into Church, I found myself in churches that I now believe had an improper theology of repentance. When the priority of repentance is turning from sin, it can produce legalism. Legalism can produce a message of guilt, condemnation, and performance-based living. In this theology, leaders are preaching to the surface cleaning. This understanding produces believers who never feel worthy, begin to have a relationship with Christ that is works-based, and never produce the fruit God designed for us to live in.

On the contrary, there is biblical repentance, which places the priority on turning *to* Christ and secondarily to turning *away* from sinful behavior. This may seem like semantics, but the effect is profound. Many times, people are attempting to turn away from behavior but have never agreed with God or His Word. Turning to Christ and agreeing with His Word are essential to experience the deep clean and will bring about long-term fruit.

I love the old hymn lyrics to "Turn Your Eyes Upon Jesus." The hymn writer Helen Lemmel understood the principle of biblical repentance. When we see Jesus, believe His Word, and turn to him in faith, the "turning" is still difficult at times; but this will be effective in producing long-lasting fruit. In so much of the Church, repentance has become a seldom-used word, either ignored because of the negative connotations and unbiblical theology or the focus on the external behavior. Neither of these two options bring about real change. Biblical repentance is such an integral aspect of powerful preaching.

The Woman at the Well

"'If you knew the gift of God, and who it is that is saying to you, *Give me a drink*, you would have asked him, and he would have given you living water'" (John 4:10). Jesus has this insightful conversation with a Samaritan woman we know was born in sin, has lived a life of sin being married five times, and is presently in disobedience while living with a man. Yet Jesus focuses on her need to have a revelation of Christ and to understand the incredible life in the kingdom that He has to offer. This is the primary emphasis in gospel preaching: to acknowledge the greatness and glory of Christ, to embrace an unshakable kingdom, and to move from darkness to light. Once the woman at the well understands Who Jesus the Messiah is in His glory, she leaves her waterpot and begins to share her life-changing experience. Yes, changing her lifestyle would be necessary and may have been filled with challenges; but once her eyes are opened to Jesus and His Word, the change would be life-altering.

This captures the essence of biblical repentance preaching. Preaching with power will transform individuals, churches, and communities, as it happened in the village of Sychar near Jacob's well. Biblical repentance always produces life, strength, and supernatural power. This deep clean Jesus wants to effect in the lives of His followers is only available through repentance. Seeing the truth in Christ and understanding His will, purposes, and glory will always be foundational in becoming a disciple. As Acts 3:19-20 says, "Repent therefore, and turn back, that your sins may be blotted out, that times of refreshing may come from the presence of the Lord."

A Culture of Repentance

In Matthew 13, Jesus shares the well-known parable on the sower. Jesus is the Sower. When we preach on a stage or individually, we are proclaiming His message. Many times, the preacher makes the mistake of acting as the sower. In truth, we are only an echo of Christ and His Word. We have no ability to produce a harvest aside from Christ and His Word.

The seed is the unchanging Word of God from Heaven. The culture and values of this world are constantly changing from culture to culture and generation to generation, but the Word of God is eternal. The seed sometimes falls by the wayside in stony places or thorns and never produces a harvest. The seed that produces a harvest is the seed that goes into fertile soil. In the fertile soil, the Word goes deep; the roots go deep; and the fruit multiplies. The significance, of course, is that the Sower is important, and the seed is crucial. However, the Word can be proclaimed in truth; but if the soil is not able to receive the Word, there will never be thirty, sixty, and hundred-fold harvests.

The point is that individuals can show up every week to church and hear biblical messages delivered by men of God; but if the soil of the heart is not soft, tender, and able to receive the Word, there will never be the fruit of a changed life. The foundation of a culture of repentance has become such a lacking element of the Western church and many other places in the days we live. As a spiritual leader, it is vital that we cultivate an atmosphere of humility, sincere desire for God's Word, and an awe of His presence so that the soil will be soft. The Old Testament prophets cry out, "Break up your fallow ground" (Jer. 4:3; Hosea 10:12). It is in proper soil that God can produce supernatural results.

We are called to preach in power. God's Word is necessary to have effective preaching. The presence of God through the Holy Spirit is essential to powerful preaching. Preaching repentance is foundational but, many times, is not emphasized. A culture of repentance will create soil that can receive the Word and produce eternal fruit. As John Milton wrote in his poem *Paradise Lost,* "Repentance is the golden key that opens the palace of eternity."

Pastors and kingdom leaders, I want to encourage you to continue to preach an uncompromising truth that refuses to bend to the culture and values of our society. It is impossible to preach the gospel message without a central focus on biblical repentance. Jesus began to preach by saying, "Repent!" Biblical repentance that emphasizes the "turning to Christ" as the priority and then "turning from sin" is the key that unlocks the door to the palace of eternity. As we preach with power together under the Lordship of Christ, we will believe God to bring a spiritual awakening.

Chapter 10
Preaching with Power

R. T. Kendall

How do preachers teach with power and spiritual authority?
And what defines power from the pulpit? There are three ways you
may be unknowingly blocking the Spirit's authority in your preaching.
There are also potential pitfalls you can fall into with your pursuit
of seeing lives touched through your sermons.

In 1 Thessalonians 1:5, Paul says, "Our gospel came to you not only in word, but also in power and in the Holy Spirit and with full conviction. You know what kind of men we proved to be among you for your sake." It is my view that when Paul says, "Our gospel did not come *only in word,*" he is admitting to the possibility of preaching the Word and not having the power of the Spirit.

The same can be seen in 1 Corinthians 2:2-4, where Paul says, "For I decided to know nothing among you except Jesus Christ and him crucified. And I was with you in weakness and in fear and much trembling, and my speech and my message were not in plausible words of wisdom, but in demonstration of the Spirit and of power." Paul is saying that when he was preaching in Corinth and Thessalonica, he had both the Word *and* the Spirit in great measure.

I hold to the view that in the Church throughout the world today, there has been a silent divorce between the Word and the Spirit. In this divorce, you have those who are on the Word side and those who are on the Spirit side. For those of us who represent the Word, the message is, "We need to know the Bible. We need to get back to expository preaching and revive 'justification by faith alone.' We must preach the sovereignty of God. Until we get back to sound preaching and sound theology like this, the honor of God's name will not be restored." What's wrong with that emphasis? Nothing! It's exactly right, in my opinion.

As for those on the Spirit side, their message is, "We need to get back to the book of Acts, where there were signs, wonders, miracles, and gifts of the Holy Spirit in operation. When they prayed, the place was shaken. Get into Peter's shadow, and you were healed. Lie to the Holy Spirit, and you're struck dead. Until we have power like that, the honor of God's name will not be restored." What's wrong with that emphasis? Nothing! It's exactly right. It's what I believe.

While both sides of the divide are correct, churches typically choose one or the other. There are churches where you've got both the Word and the Spirit together, and I thank God for those. But they are the exception. They are rare. It is possible to hold firm to both beliefs, though. I'm not saying I know how to do that. I wish I did. I wish I could say with Paul, "Our gospel did not come to you in word only, but also in power, and in the Holy Spirit."

If I were totally honest, looking back at twenty-five years at Westminster Chapel, I preached with the power of the Holy Spirit anointing only twice. The first time, I was preaching a message from Philippians 1:12, where the apostle Paul said, "I want you to know, brothers, that what has happened to me has really served to advance the gospel." For some reason, on that day, I had power like I had never experienced. And when it was over and I prayed and sat down, I thought, *Well, today I had it.* The place was electric. There was total silence. But everybody knew I had preached with the power of the Spirit that day.

An hour later, one of our deacons came to me and said, "I've got some disappointing news. The man who does the recordings was ill, and he forgot to call in. Your sermon was not recorded."

I was so disappointed. One of the other deacons suggested that I just preach the same message the next week at Bromley. I thought it was a good idea, and so I did. I had the same outline and the same words, but the message fell flat. It wasn't even worth recording.

There was one other time I preached with unusual power. That Sunday morning, I preached to two or three thousand at Coral Ridge Presbyterian Church in Fort Lauderdale. It was an ornate liturgical service, and I preached a sermon that I had preached dozens of times. It went well. But later that day, I took a flight to Bimini in the Bahamas, where I had planned to go fishing. My fishing guide, a gentleman known as Bonefish Sam, was also a pastor; and he asked me to preach at his church that Sunday evening.

When we walked in, there were just twenty Bahamians on their knees, praying. I thought, *Lord, what would You like to say to these people?* Hebrews 13:8 came to my mind: "Jesus Christ is the same yesterday and today and forever." In a moment, I had a sense of God like I've not had for a long time. I could see Jesus! I went up and preached in a way neither I nor those twenty Bahamians will ever forget.

I thought, *Lord, why didn't You let me preach like this at Westminster Chapel? Why couldn't I have had this same anointing this morning when I preached to thousands in Fort Lauderdale? And when I go back to Westminster Chapel, why can't I have this then? Instead, You give it to a handful of men and women who aren't the movers and shakers of the world. Yet I was given the power to preach to them.*

I wish I knew how to make it happen, but I don't. I've had good training. I've been to seminary. I've had classes in homiletics. I had Dr. Martyn

Lloyd-Jones as a tutor, arguably the greatest preacher since Charles Spurgeon! Every Thursday, we spent two hours together. I would go over my sermons for the following weekend with him, and he helped me. Imagine having a teacher like that! I'm much better as a result of Dr. Lloyd-Jones taking me under his wing.

But to preach with power, you cannot *make* it happen. Still, I will give you my best and share with you on what I would call "experimental preaching." You might think I mean "experiential preaching." That would miss the mark. We're talking about an experiment.

My thesis is that the Holy Spirit wants to reach the people to whom you and I speak. But will the Holy Spirit get through us and use us so we are an instrument? Or will we block the Holy Spirit?

Here is a story from church history that will help illustrate this idea. John Calvin wrote a letter to Martin Luther, thinking he could get his view about the Lord's Supper across to Luther. After Luther's assistant, Philip Melanchthon, read the letter, he would not let Luther see it. Melanchthon intercepted the letter, saying that the aged Luther was too frail. He wouldn't be able to cope with Calvin's letter.

In the same way, you and I could intercept or block the Spirit from reaching the people. It's an assumption that what we need more than anything in the world is the anointing of the Spirit. First John 2:20 says, "But you have been anointed by the Holy One, and you all have knowledge." And 1 John 2:27 says, "The anointing that you received." In both cases, John uses the same Greek word, translated as anointing.

The word *anointing* comes from the same word that we get Christ from. It's from the root word *chrió*, which means smearing as with an ointment. Jesus is the Anointed One. He is the Messiah. *That* is the kind of anointing we would want.

There are also other words in Greek that may seem to be that anointing. There is the word *charismata*, meaning "grace gift." There are those who want the gifts of grace. To them, that would be the anointing they desire. God alone can give these. But this kind of anointing is not what I believe we need to be preaching in the power of the Spirit. *Charismata* is not from the same root as *chrió*. The English transliteration may be similar, but these words are not the same.

There's also another Greek word, *charisma*, which may also sound like it could refer to the same anointing as *chrió*; but it does not. It has a different root altogether. *Charisma* refers to one's natural gift, your personality. It is, indeed, a gift of God if you have real charisma. The trouble is that you could have charisma in the flesh. There are those who aspire to have charisma in the pulpit. It seems to be the only thing they want—to have something that will make people think they're great or different.

This certainly is not what I am talking about as the anointing we need, the kind of anointing that will enable you and me to radiate the Word of Christ and to radiate Jesus. So we speak in such a way that the power of the Holy Spirit gets past us, and people are suddenly aware that God is speaking. *That* is the kind of power we should want.

There are several Greek words that could be taken to refer to that kind of anointing. On the day of Pentecost, Peter used the word *parousia*, meaning boldness or confidence.[1] Peter was full of that. The amazing thing is that six weeks before, Peter had denied knowing Jesus! You would think that he would be the last person God would give *parousia* and use on the day of Pentecost. But Peter was a forgiven man, and it goes to show that God uses forgiven people. On the day of Pentecost, there was not a bit of self-righteousness in Peter. He was aware of how unworthy he was. He was not up there preaching because he thought, *I'm ready. I have been obedient.* No, he was aware of how unworthy he was.

I believe that is a key for all of us to realize that if God uses us, we have this power in "jars of clay, to show that the surpassing power belongs to God

---

1   Acts 2:14-41

and not to us" (2 Cor. 4:7). That was true of Peter. But there was another thing Peter had on that day. Acts 1:8 says, "But you will receive power when the Holy Spirit has come upon you." The Greek word for power here is *dynamin*, where we get the word *dynamite*. Acts 2:4 talks about the Holy Spirit coming, and people were speaking in other languages "as the Spirit gave them utterance." It wasn't them speaking; it was God doing it.

Interestingly, the Greek word for *utterance* is turned into the verb form when it refers to when Peter addressed the crowd in Acts 2:14. Peter was preaching in his own language but with the same power as what enabled the crowds to speak in tongues. This is an unusual power that we can certainly pray and hope for. And we certainly don't want to intercept the Spirit. We don't want to stop the Spirit from coming.

Would you like your words to flow through you uninterrupted so that the people are confronted by God, by unusual power, by the anointing? If you're a football fan, you may know that Vince Lombardi was probably the greatest football coach ever. He won more games than anybody. When Lombardi was asked what his secret was, he said, "It's very simple. Winning is not the main thing; it's the only thing."

I would say the same about this kind of power. It is the only thing we should desire.

Being aware that we have access to such power, we should aspire to preach with Word and power. We should also be mindful not to block the Spirit.

How Do We Block the Spirit?

Is it important to you to get a good word so the intellectual person out there will say it's good? Are you after finding a colorful phrase? There are those for whom that's all they want—the wisdom of words. You can aspire to that, but I guarantee you that you will not be preaching with power. If you want some advice on this point, listen to Charles Spurgeon, who was arguably the greatest preacher of all time. Spurgeon said, "Labor to be plain."[2] That should rob you of any ambition to be eloquent so people will hang on to your words.

Years ago, I took a friend of mine to hear Dr. Martyn Lloyd-Jones preach. He preached with great power. It just so happened that he was also very able with words.

When Lloyd-Jones finished preaching, I was thinking, *Oh, that was marvelous. I felt the presence of God.*

But all my friend said was, "Not one dangling participle or a split infinitive!" That's what he got out of the sermon. Dr. Lloyd-Jones would never have wanted to impress my friend in the first place.

There are those who want to have the carefully worded phrase, and *that* is what matters to them. Go back to what Spurgeon said about laboring to be plain and to what Paul said in 1 Corinthians 1:17: "For Christ did not send me to baptize but to preach the gospel, and not with words of eloquent wisdom, lest the cross of Christ be emptied of its power."

If you make it your goal to sound good and impress the intellectual, you will rob Christ of the glory. You will speak in such a way that the power of the cross is lost. I'll give you three bits of advice to wrap this up:

1. Don't try to be eloquent.
2. Don't try to be eloquent.
3. Don't try to be eloquent.

That is one way in which you will block the Spirit—by seeking words that will sound good.

We also block the Spirit when we pervert the text. Sadly, so much preaching today is motivational with preachers simply bringing in the Bible

---

2   Charles Spurgeon, "Forward," in "An All-Around Ministry: Addresses to Ministers and Students," Bible Bulletin Board, Accessed September 8, 2024, https://www.biblebb.com/files/spurgeon/aarm02.htm.

to support their message. Don't do that. Be unashamed of the Scripture. Read the Scripture. Unfold it so the pure Word of God is being passed on. Do not pervert the text. Do not change it to sound the way you want it to sound. Do not come up with a meaning that you hope. Instead, labor until you find the answer to what the original author meant by these words. Then, be willing to preach it, even if it contradicts what you hoped it would say. Until you've done that work, you're not ready to preach a passage.

The Spirit can also be blocked when we copy others. We've all done this. Over the years, many of us find a hero; and then we try to sound like they do. When you imitate another person, you will never capture their genius. You'll only pick up habits they might have.

Many years ago, there was a preacher in Texas who had an eccentric habit. Whenever he began to preach and it seemed he was preaching with great authority, he would cup his left ear with his left hand and would keep on preaching. Nobody knew why he did it. Well, that man became the professor of preaching at Southwestern Baptist Theological Seminary (SWBTS) in Fort Worth, Texas. And you could always tell if someone had been a student of his. When they thought they were preaching with authority, their left hand would come up over their ear as they continued preaching. A lot of people thought these young preachers were great. They sounded just like their professor.

Years later, I had the privilege of speaking at SWBTS; and I told them that story.

An old professor came up to me afterward and said, "I know exactly who you're talking about." He gave me the name, and it was indeed to whom I was referring.

So I asked this man, "Why did he cup his ear with his left hand?"

Turns out that the other professor had been hard of hearing. When he cupped his ear, he could hear better. Everybody else thought it was the anointing!

Dr. Lloyd-Jones told me a similar story. Many years ago in Wales, there was a preacher who had an eccentric habit that when he preached, his hair would get down in his eyes. Instead of taking his hand and pushing his hair back, he would shake it back with a flick of his head. Sure enough, there were young preachers all over Wales who, as they preached, would periodically flick their heads, even if they were bald!

But even if you imitate a brilliant preacher, you will never capture their genius. When I first started preaching, I, too, tried to mimic my pastor. It was silly. I couldn't preach like him, but I tried. I used to try to imitate others, too. I'm ashamed to say it took years before I realized that I am the way God made me, and I simply began to be myself. If people don't like me, they don't like me. But I'll be myself. When you are yourself rather than trying to imitate someone else, you begin to honor God because, after all, He's the one who made you like this. You are honoring God when you are just yourself.

The Spirit is also blocked when we avoid certain Scriptures. Let's say you're preaching through a chapter or a book of the Bible, which is what I did at Westminster Chapel. As you go through a chapter, there will be a verse in there that you'll think, *Oh, I don't like what it says. I don't want to preach on that.* When you avoid a Scripture just because it doesn't cohere with your theology, you will be blocking the Spirit and robbing the people of what God wanted them to hear. Be willing to unfold the Scripture, even if it hits you.

When we let our personal feelings get involved, we may block the Spirit. I'm sorry to say that I've done this, but I'm sure we've all allowed our feelings to cloud our minds. Let's say there's somebody that you've had a controversy with, or there's a personality clash, or they've been troublemakers. While preparing your sermon, you look for something that will reach them. I'll tell you what will happen when you do that. You won't reach them at all. Your motive is not good. Don't ever do that.

As preachers, we ought to be instruments of God in the pulpit. When people hear and see us, they must forget we are there; they should just see

God. It's like a clear glass window through which they can see what's on the other side, forgetting there's glass there. If there's a crack in the window, though, people focus on the crack, not on what's on the other side. We become cracked windows and block the Spirit when we avoid preaching just what the Scripture says and let our feelings get involved. We sometimes also aim to be a stained-glass window—not meant to be seen through but meant to draw attention—when we focus on words of wisdom and try to be eloquent, pervert the text, or we copy others. We ought to be like a clear glass window.

Sometimes, we preach in ways that block the Spirit. There are several ways of preaching that get in the way of preaching with power. One would be preaching *for* the people. That would be performance, trying to be a stained-glass window. Next, there is preaching *at* the people. That's where you have a grudge, and you take it to the pulpit. The pulpit is not yours any more than the communion table is yours. It's the Lord's table. You're not there to use the pulpit to get at people.

Third, there's preaching *down at* the people. That would be arrogance, where you're just looking down at them. People can tell if you're doing that, so don't. There's also preaching *up to* the people. That's cowardice to be thinking, *Who am I to be preaching to these people?* Don't do that. But when we are preaching *to* the people, a Divine transaction takes place where you're letting God speak. You're fearless, and you're just preaching what they need.

When we block the Spirit, we grieve the Holy Spirit. In Ephesians 4:30, Paul says, "Do not grieve the Holy Spirit of God, by whom you were sealed for the day of redemption." The word *grieve* comes from the Greek word *lypeite*, meaning to get your feelings hurt. In other words, the Holy Spirit is sensitive. He can get his feelings hurt. He can be grieved.

How do we grieve the Spirit? Paul addresses that right after he says *not* to grieve the Holy Spirit of God. He says, "Let all bitterness and wrath and anger and clamor and slander be put away from you, along with all malice.

Be kind to one another, tenderhearted, forgiving one another, as God in Christ forgave you" (Eph. 4:31-32).

I have written a book and spoken on the topic of total forgiveness and won't go into detail here.[3] I'll just say this much: the darkest hour of my life for my wife Louise and I happened when we were at Westminster Chapel years ago. What had happened was unjust, wrong, and unfair. And I was angry. I was bitter.

Joseph, an old friend from Romania, happened to be in London. And because I knew he wouldn't tell anybody, I shared with Joseph what had happened. I thought he would put his arm around me and say, "R. T., you have every right to be angry. Get it out of your system." That's what I wanted.

Instead, Joseph looked at me and said, "R. T., you must totally forgive them. Until you totally forgive them, you will be in chains. Release them, and you will be released."

My twenty-five years in London could be boiled down to this fifteen-minute encounter. Nobody had ever talked to me like that in my life. "Faithful *are* the wounds of a friend" (Prov. 27:6). Joseph's words changed my life. It changed me, and it changed my preaching. The Bible began to open up to me. I had more ideas for books than I ever had in my life—more than I ever dreamed I would have.

You may say, "Well, in my case, you don't know what I've gone through." If you have suffered more than anybody you've ever met, in your church, or in your country and if it can be proved that nobody has suffered like you, then you might say, "God wouldn't expect me to forgive that. He understands." I have news for you. God will not bend the rules for you, just like He didn't bend the rules for me. You must not harbor bitterness and unforgiveness. There are no exceptions.

Instead, if you've suffered much, the angels have a word for you: congratulations! Oh, yes! If you've suffered like *that* and then you forgive *that*,

---

3   R. T. Kendall, *Total Forgiveness* (Lake Mary: Charisma House, 2007).

you have a promise of blessing that nobody around you would have. Take it with both hands and thank God for it because that will change you. It will enable you to preach with more clarity.

When it comes to preaching with power, you cannot expect to have such power as long as there's *any* unforgiveness in your life, as long as you're holding a grudge. I don't care what it is or how bad someone was to you. Until you forgive, you will not know what it's like to experience the "ungrieved" Holy Spirit.

We're told in John 1:32 that John the Baptist knew that Jesus was the Messiah because the dove came down and just stayed. I believe that when the dove came down on Jesus, he stayed because Jesus never grieved the Spirit—not even once. We must pray for the Spirit to rest upon us because there's no bitterness there. For you to preach with the ungrieved Spirit means that the Spirit will master your preparation.

✚

This is embarrassing to share, but it might be a blessing to someone. When I was at Westminster, I started my morning sermon preparation on Monday morning. For six days, I would prepare for Sunday; but I also had to preach on Thursdays and Fridays. I had to preach four new sermons a week. I had to have the ungrieved Spirit. So, I always started preparing on Monday mornings.

Only once in twenty-five years did I head out unprepared. I was out preaching all over Britain, and I hadn't cracked a book! I hadn't prepared. I knew the verse I was going to use, but I wasn't ready.

By Saturday morning, I thought, *Oh, Lord, please help me. I haven't prepared all week. Please forgive me for what I've done, and please make up for these days I had lost.*

I will never forget it. It was nine in the morning, and I prayed that we would have a whole day—no interruptions, no phone calls, nobody knocking at the door. But about that time, Louise and I got into an argument. I slammed the door, went to my desk, took my Bible, and said, "Now, Lord, give me something! Give me something. Also, deal with that woman. Now, Lord, help me find something. Show me what to say."

Ten o'clock: a blank sheet of paper. Eleven, twelve, one, two o'clock. A blank sheet of paper. I had nothing.

"Lord, please help me," I begged. "You know what I say tomorrow will go all over the world. You've got to help me."

I didn't get any help at all.

At four that afternoon, I went to the kitchen. There was Louise, standing by the refrigerator. She was in tears.

I said, "Honey, I'm sorry. It was all my fault."

"Well," she said, "it's partly my fault."

"No, it was all my fault," I assured her. "And I am sorry."

We kissed. We hugged. I went back to the same desk, same Bible, same blank sheet of paper. But this time, I couldn't write my thoughts fast enough. In forty-five minutes, I had everything I needed for Sunday. What normally would take several days took just forty-five minutes that day.

You see, when the ungrieved Spirit comes down, you get more done than you could—even in years. You need the ungrieved Spirit in your preparation; and then, when you preach, you need to preach with the power of that ungrieved Spirit. When you preach, be willing to veer off your notes as the Spirit leads. Be willing to say what is necessary. Aristotle said that public speakers need *ethos*, *pathos*, and *logos*. *Ethos* refers to the credibility of the speaker, *pathos* to the senses of the audience and having a certain passion as you preach. And *logos* refers to content, reason, and logic.

When the Holy Spirit comes in great power, you will have *ethos*, *pathos*, and *logos* without trying. The anointing will be there, and you will be preaching as before the audience of One. You won't be trying to please anybody out there. You will preach in a way that pleases God alone.

Chapter 11

Preaching for the Glory of Christ

Joshua West

The primary reason we preach is in declaration and proclamation of the glory of Christ. Yes, we hope that the lost will believe and be saved; yes, we want the believer to hear and cling to the promises of God; and yes, we want to see our Christian brothers and sisters walk in faith, victory, and freedom. But we preach the truth of Christ as revealed to us in the Scripture primarily because He is worthy of all glory.

Second Timothy 4:1-2 says, "I charge you in the presence of God and of Christ Jesus, who is to judge the living and the dead, and by his appearing and his kingdom: preach the word; be ready in season and out of season; reprove, rebuke, and exhort, with complete patience and teaching." We live in a time where the pulpits of many, if not most evangelical churches in our culture are man-centered and theologically shallow. Often, the sermons that come out of these churches are more like motivational speeches or TED talks, rather than biblically sound sermons. These men are full of selfish ambition and are teaching the people who follow them to also be full of selfish ambition. Now, more than ever, we need men of conviction, who know and fear the Lord, have no fear of man, are deaf to criticism from the world but also deaf to the applause of men, whose hearts have been set aflame by the Word of God, and who preach for the glory of Christ alone.

Galatians 1:10 says, "For am I now seeking the approval of man, or of God? Or am I trying to please man? If I were still trying to please man, I would not be a servant of Christ." To be of any real benefit to the people to whom we preach, we must be utterly convinced of the truth and power of the Word of God. You cannot effectively minister to someone to whom you are pandering or trying to please. The only preaching that truly has any real power to affect and change the lives of people, is the preaching of God's Word under the anointing of the Holy Spirit. No matter how worldly wise or practical our words are, they have no power to truly penetrate the heart, regenerate the heart, renew the mind, or conform us to the image of Christ.

The only message worth living for is one that is worth dying for. Jesus said, "Whoever would save his life will lose it, but whoever loses his life for my sake will find it" (Matt. 16:25). As preachers of the gospel, we have been entrusted with the very words of God—words of judgment and power, that can make dead bones live again and bring salvation and eternal life to all who by faith repent and believe. Where are the preachers who truly believe this—men of faith who preach with the weight of eternity on their shoulders and the fear of the Lord in their hearts?

"Thus says the LORD: 'Heaven is my throne, and the earth is my footstool; what is the house that you would build for me, and what is the place of my rest? All these things my hand has made, and so all these things came to be, declares the LORD. But this is the one to whom I will look: he who is humble and contrite in spirit and trembles at my word'" (Isa. 66:1-2).

When the apostle Paul penned the words of the second epistle to Timothy, he was sitting in a place that had become too familiar to him, a jail cell. But this stint in jail would be different than all the other times he had been arrested for proclaiming the gospel because it would be the last time—not because they finally convinced him to stop preaching or because Rome's position on the Christian religion had changed but because at the end of this stint in jail, he would be beheaded and become a martyr for the glory of Christ and the message of the gospel.

It's also apparent that as he wrote this letter, he knew his death was imminent because of what he says at the end of chapter four: "For I am already being poured out as a drink offering, and the time of my departure has come. I have fought the good fight, I have finished the race, I have kept the faith. Henceforth there is laid up for me the crown of righteousness, which the Lord, the righteous judge, will award to me on that day, and not only to me but also to all who have loved his appearing" (2 Tim. 4:6-8).

Timothy was a young pastor who was like a son to the apostle Paul, and it is apparent that he loved him dearly. Paul had mentored, trained, and raised up Timothy as a pastor and apparently had known him since his youth. So, knowing Paul's love for Timothy and knowing that he was aware of his impending death make the words Paul chooses to write Timothy under the inspiration of the Holy Spirit feel so much more urgent and profound.

If you knew that you were about to be killed and had the opportunity to write one last letter to your son in the faith, what would it say? The context and conditions surrounding the writing of the letter of 2 Timothy are so important to understand to help us see with clarity the weight of Paul's statements. In the most grandiose way possible, Paul prefaces the command he gives Timothy to "preach the word" by reminding him that his life and ministry are lived out in the presence of God and in view of Christ, Who will one day judge everyone. In 2 Timothy 4:1-2, we read, "I charge you in the presence of God and of Christ Jesus, who is to judge the living and the dead, and by his appearing and his kingdom: preach the word."

What an intense way to start a statement. Paul says, "I charge you." This phrase could also be translated, as "I command you." It is apparent that this is a very serious command of the utmost importance. This is seemingly the most important thing said in the entire epistle; we can make this assumption because of the emphasis put on the statement. Make sure, above all else, that you proclaim the words of Scripture with sincerity and integrity. Remember it was because of his bold and fearless proclamation of the Scripture that Paul was sentenced to die. It was a message worth dying for because it is a message that brings eternal life to all who believe. Why then would we ever treat the Scriptures with any less reverence than this? People have bled and died for the sake of preserving the Scripture and for proclaiming the Scripture; and this is because they are the very words of God filled with truth and life.

We are to preach the very words of God! Like Moses and the prophets of the Old Testament, John the Baptist, Jesus, and all of the apostles, we preach, "Thus saith the Lord!" And in this line of faithfulness to the clear and bold proclamation of the Word of the Lord, Paul commands Timothy to simply preach what God has revealed to us in Scripture. Because when we add anything to the word of the Lord and the gospel of Jesus Christ, we rob it of its power. Our words, opinions, and worldly wisdom literally dilute the power of the Scripture.

As Paul says to the Corinthians, "For Christ did not send me to baptize but to preach the gospel, and not with words of eloquent wisdom, lest the cross of Christ be emptied of its power" (1 Cor. 1:17). With great emphasis and passion, Paul commands Timothy and every true preacher of Christ who would come after him to preach the Word of God because Paul knew that a time was coming when people would reject sound doctrine and raise up teachers who would instead preach what the people want to hear—smooth and easy messages aimed at pleasing the flesh and void of the message of repentance and the fullness of the gospel. And because of this void, their messages are void of any real power to transform hearts and lives. But these preachers and their messages are deceptive because they seem godly when, in fact, they are hollow and damning to the soul. In 2 Timothy 3:5, Paul says that these people will have a form of godliness while "denying its power." He says to "avoid such people." Instead, in 2 Timothy 4:2-5, he says:

> Preach the word; be ready in season and out of season; reprove, rebuke, and exhort, with complete patience and teaching. For the time is coming when people will not endure sound teaching, but having itching ears they will accumulate for themselves teachers to suit their own passions, and will turn away from listening to the truth and wander off into myths. As for you, always be sober-minded, endure suffering, do the work of an evangelist, fulfill your ministry.

We are commanded, as ministers of the gospel, to preach the Word; and Paul says we are to do it when it's in season when the culture applauds, people accept it, and they are saying amen. But he also says we are commanded to preach the Word when it is out of season. When they tell us it's unloving or inappropriate and put us in jail for it and when they won't listen to us. We must be sober-minded, endure suffering, do the work of an evangelist, and discharge the duties of our ministry.

Biblical Preaching

Since God has commanded us to preach the Word, it is important that we clearly define what that means. As preachers called by God, our preaching should be centered around the Scripture. The trouble is most people who stand behind a pulpit in evangelical churches in the West today would claim that they are preaching the Word. The question we must ask ourselves is whether God is using us to preach His Word or whether we are using God to preach *our* word.

Before we can define what biblical preaching is, we must define what it is not. Biblical preaching is not using God's Word to validate some idea, system, or philosophy you have. Biblical preaching is not a church growth scheme.

It's not trying to preach what you think and what people want to hear. It's not your opinion or personal testimony, although your testimony can be used as a small anecdotal example. It is not anything superimposed onto the text. The Bible is not a garnish for your meal of words. Biblical preaching is proclamation, explanation, and application of God's Word.

Biblical preaching is proclaiming the whole counsel of God's Word. It is worshipful, Christ-honoring, God-exulting, and gospel-centered. All throughout the New Testament, we see preaching held up as God's prescribed method for saving those who believe, renewing the minds of His children, conforming us to the image of Christ, and declaring the glory of Christ, the King above all kings and Lord above all lords.

In Mark 16:15, we read that Jesus said, "'Go into all the world and proclaim the gospel to the whole creation.'" Paul continued Jesus' teaching in 1 Corinthians 1:20-24:

> Where is the one who is wise? Where is the scribe? Where is the debater of this age? Has not God made foolish the wisdom of the world? For since, in the wisdom of God, the world did not know God through wisdom, it pleased God through the folly of what we preach to save those who believe. For Jews demand signs and Greeks seek wisdom, but we preach Christ crucified, a stumbling block to Jews and folly to Gentiles, but to those who are called, both Jews and Greeks, Christ the power of God and the wisdom of God.

Biblical preaching should either correct, rebuke, or encourage; it can have many purposes in the life of the believer. It is a warning of coming judgment and condemnation, and it brings salvation to all who believe. It is filled with unbreakable promises and assurances. And while there are many things that result from the preaching of God's Word, the main purpose of preaching is that of declaration and proclamation. The Greek word κηρύσσω (kērússō) is often translated as "preach" in some English translations of the New Testament, but it is also translated in many versions as "proclaim." The main reason we preach above all other reasons is that the Word of the Lord must be proclaimed for the glory of Christ our King.

Preaching the Whole Counsel of God

After spending much of the first seven chapters of Romans explaining to us that none are good (Rom. 3:10-12), that "the wages of sin is death" (Rom. 6:23), and that "all have sinned and fallen short of the glory of God" (Rom. 3:23), Paul shifts from preaching and applying the law to preaching the gospel of salvation that comes by grace through faith in Christ alone (Eph. 2:8). Paul understood for those to whom he was speaking to be able to understand their need for grace and salvation, he had to apply the law so they would understand that apart from Christ, all are subject to eternal judgment and condemnation; and so are we.

Paul says in Romans 8:1-4:

> There is therefore now no condemnation for those who are in Christ Jesus. For the law of the Spirit of life has set you free in Christ Jesus from the law of sin and death. For God has done what the law, weakened by the flesh, could not do. By sending his own Son in the likeness of sinful flesh and for sin, he condemned sin in the flesh, in order that the righteous requirement of the law might be fulfilled in us, who walk not according to the flesh but according to the Spirit.

Paul preached the Law of Moses and the proclamation of the prophets to magnify the beauty, power, and supremacy of Christ. We must preach each part of the Bible in light of the rest of the Bible. We must preach the New Testament in light of the Old Testament and the Old Testament in light of the New. We must preach the gospel in light of the Law and prophets, and we must preach the Law and prophets in light of the gospel. Everything in the Bible and really everything in the universe is merely context and background meant to magnify and glorify Jesus Christ and His glorious gospel of grace, and our preaching of His Word is no different. In Revelation 5:9-10, we read, "And they sang a new song, saying, 'Worthy are you to take the scroll and to open its seals, for you were slain, and by your blood you ransomed people for God from every tribe and language and people and nation, and you have made them a kingdom and priests to our God, and they shall reign on the earth.'"

We must preach the whole counsel of God from the Old and New Testament and treat every part as sacred, holy, and worthy of preaching, because "all Scripture is breathed out by God and profitable for teaching, for reproof, for correction, and for training in righteousness, that the man of God may be complete, equipped for every good work" (2 Tim. 3:16-17).

The Beautiful Feet of the Gospel

In Romans chapter ten, Paul comes to a mountaintop moment in his message when he declares in verse thirteen that "'everyone who calls on the name of the Lord will be saved.'" Because Paul preached the whole counsel of God's Word, his gospel message was powerful and compelling. The law brings us to despair and shows us that apart from salvation through Christ, we are hopeless. Simply telling people God loves them and can save them is not enough. For the grace of God to be seen for the amazing gift that it is, we must labor in preaching the holiness of God and the fact that He cannot co-exist with sin. We must labor to preach about the sinfulness of man and the grievousness of sin so that when we preach the gospel of grace, it raises Christ up in His rightful place as King above all, the Lord of all things, and the exclusive means by which men are saved.

Paul makes a powerful proclamation about Christ on behalf of Christ first and foremost, in honor of Christ, and then that those who hear his message might believe and be saved. Paul then makes a powerful plea for biblical preaching and that other biblical preachers would rise up and make proclamation in service of the Savior King in Romans 10:

How then will they call on him in whom they have not believed? And how are they to believe in him of whom they have never heard? And how are they to hear without someone preaching? And how are they to preach unless they are sent? As it is written, "How beautiful are the feet of those who preach the good news!" But they have not all obeyed the gospel. For Isaiah says, "Lord, who has believed what he has heard from us?" So faith comes from hearing, and hearing through the word of Christ (Rom. 10:14-17).

Here Paul is using progressive logic that exposes the importance of his message, the need for biblical preaching, and the need for biblical preachers to proclaim the truth of the Scripture, with the message of the gospel always as the centerpiece. After making this passionate plea for biblical preaching, he quotes from Isaiah 52:

"Therefore my people shall know my name. Therefore in that day they shall know that it is I who speak; here I am." How beautiful upon the mountains are the feet of him who brings good news, who publishes peace, who brings good news of happiness, who publishes salvation, who says to Zion, "Your God reigns." The voice of your watchmen—they lift up their voice; together they sing for joy; for eye to eye they see the return of the LORD to Zion. Break forth together into singing, you waste places of Jerusalem, for the LORD has comforted his people; he has redeemed Jerusalem. The LORD has bared his holy arm before the eyes of all the nations and all the ends of the earth shall see the salvation of our God (Isa. 52:6-10).

This prophetic passage from Scripture gives a foreshadowing of the salvation that Christ would bring; and then in chapter fifty-three, Isaiah paints a picture of Who the Savior would be and what He would go through to accomplish it.

This is a picture of a kingdom that is internally at war; and eventually, the rightful King is victorious, and the war is over. Although in the city, there is now peace and the King is sitting on His throne ruling and reigning, the battle is still raging on the mountaintops and in the valleys. The war is over, and the King is victorious; but the people spread out across the land fighting don't know it yet. So, the King sends out heralds to proclaim the message of peace and salvation to all who surrender to His Lordship. What makes this Great King so amazing is that although the war is over and He rightfully could destroy all of the enemies that lived in rebellion against Him, instead, He has sent out heralds to make a declaration of peace and salvation. If they will lay down their swords, renounce their rebellion, and surrender to the King, He will not only, in mercy, pardon their sins and not give them what they deserve, which is condemnation; but in His amazing grace, He will give them something that they don't deserve and could never earn, which is sonship and a place in His kingdom.

As God's called preachers, we are these heralds! It is not our job to alter the message or to try and make it more pleasing to the person to whom we are declaring it. We do not have that right. If we change or distort the message because we fear how people will react to it, it shows we fear them more than we fear the King Who sent us. Beware of the words in Luke 9:26, "For whoever is ashamed of me and of my words, of him will the Son of Man be ashamed when he comes in his glory and the glory of the Father and of the holy angels."

If a king sent a messenger to proclaim His message to someone and that messenger altered or changed the message so that it would be more pleasing or acceptable or less offensive or harsh, that messenger would be a poor messenger. The king would be very upset and might even put this messenger to death because of his treason. We must remember as we preach that the only reason the message has power and authority is that they are the words of the King Who has all power and authority.

To herald the King's message where the battle is still raging can be dangerous; and in doing this, we might be rejected, injured, or even killed. But the message is so important that it must be proclaimed. We must also remember that the people who see us as enemies are actually the same ones we are trying to convince and persuade; these are the ones we hope will believe and be saved. "For we must all appear before the judgment seat of Christ, so that each one may receive what is due for what he has done in the body, whether good or evil. Therefore, knowing the fear of the Lord, we persuade others. But what we are is known to God, and I hope it is known also to your conscience" (2 Cor. 5:10-11).

As preachers, we do this faithfully for a few reasons. First of all, it is because we are convinced that Jesus is the victorious King and we have surrendered our lives in order that His kingdom might come, and "[His] will be done on earth as it is in heaven" (Matt. 6:10). We do this because we, too, were once enemies of God living in rebellion, and someone heralded the message of the gospel to us that we might be saved. But we do it mostly because we have been called and commanded to do so. If we faithfully present the message of the King, we have the authority and the power of the King behind us. But if we misrepresent the King or go forth with our own message, we do so without the power and authority of the King.

Preaching for the Glory of Christ

The primary reason we preach is in declaration and proclamation of the glory of Christ. Yes, we hope that the lost will believe and be saved (Acts 16:31); yes, we want the believer to hear and cling to the promises of God; and yes, we want to see our Christian brothers and sisters walk in faith, victory, and freedom. But we preach the truth of Christ as revealed to us in the Scripture, primarily because He is worthy of all glory.

Boldness for fearlessly preaching God's Word as written with conviction and power is not something that can be taught at Bible college or seminary. It is found deep in the recesses of the prayer closet; it is found in a man in whom the Word has done the work of producing reverent fear, a humble heart, and saving faith. It is found in a man who has answered the call to come and die that he might live (John 11:25), who "walk[s] by the Spirit" putting no confidence in the flesh (Gal. 5:16), who values the truth of God's Word even more than daily bread. This is a man who preaches for the glory of Christ alone and has no thought toward the opinions, power, influence, acclaim, or approval of men. As Luke 6:26 says, "'Woe to you, when all people speak well of you, for so their fathers did to the false prophets.'"

This holy boldness is not born in pride or arrogance but instead in conviction, humility, anguish, and faith. Remember that during Paul's passionate plea for biblical preaching and biblical preachers to rise up in Romans 10, he reminds us in verse seventeen, "Faith comes from hearing, and hearing through the word of Christ." So let us preach Christ as revealed in His Word. The true preacher is a man who knows God in prayer and from His Word and has answered the call to make Him known to a lost and dying world, come what may. He builds the faith of his congregation as he proclaims the promises and purposes of God to the people as he urges them to walk by faith in the word of God and not by sight (2 Cor. 5:7).

Preaching as proclamation for the glory of Christ doesn't mean that the preacher doesn't care about the people to whom he preaches; quite the opposite, he preaches Christ out of deep care and love for those to whom God has entrusted to him. He is convinced of His own weakness and convinced of the power of God's Word so much that he wouldn't dare twist, distort, or add to it. We must preach for the glory of Christ because Christ Himself said, "'And I, when I am lifted up from the earth, will draw all people to myself'" (John 12:32).

It is in realizing that we are weak and powerless as people, pastors, and preachers that we cling to the grace of Christ, understanding that it is enough. It is in this surrender that the power of Christ will rest upon you, upon your preaching, and on your ministry. We make bold proclamations because we come in the authority and power of God. As 2 Corinthians 12:9-10 says, "But he said to me, 'My grace is sufficient for you, for my power is made perfect in weakness.' Therefore I will boast all the more gladly of my weaknesses, so that the power of Christ may rest upon me. For the sake of Christ, then, I am content with weaknesses, insults, hardships, persecutions, and calamities. For when I am weak, then I am strong."

We preach the whole message of Scripture; we rightly divide and proclaim the Scripture, and we preach every part of the Scripture in light of the cross. So many preachers hold to a form of godliness but deny the substance of its power because their faith is in something other than Christ alone. The power of our preaching and the power of Christianity is in the cross, the gospel of Jesus Christ! "For I am not ashamed of the gospel, for it is the power of God for salvation to everyone who believes, to the Jew first and also to the Greek. For in it the righteousness of God is revealed from faith for faith as it is written, 'The righteous shall live by faith'" (Rom. 1:16-17).

> And I, when I came to you, brothers, did not come proclaiming to you the testimony of God with lofty speech or wisdom. For I decided to know nothing among you except Jesus Christ and him crucified. And I was with you in weakness and in fear and much trembling, and my speech and my message were not in plausible words of wisdom, but in demonstration of the Spirit and of power, so that your faith might not rest in the wisdom of me but in the power of God (1 Cor. 2:1-5).

Just like in every other area, God will not let anything take away from or diminish His glory. He downsized Gideon's army; sent Elijah to face the 450 prophets of Baal all alone; sent an Israelite boy to slay the Philistine's giant; and defeated death, Hell, and grave with His only Son because He doesn't want there to be any doubt where the power came from and where the glory belongs. And preaching is no different. It's God's Word, God's power, and God's glory.

First Corinthians 1:21-24 says, "For since, in the wisdom of God, the world did not know God through wisdom, it pleased God through the folly of what we preach to save those who believe. For Jews demand signs and Greeks seek wisdom, but we preach Christ crucified, a stumbling block to Jews and folly to Gentiles, but to those who are called, both Jews and Greeks, Christ the power of God and the wisdom of God."

When we preach the message of Christ for the glory of God, the power of Christ rests on us; and hearts and lives are changed. The lost repent; the saved are strengthened; the kingdom is forwarded; and Christ is glorified. The Spirit of God moves in a demonstration and in power when our faith rests not in the wisdom of men but in the power of God. The power of preaching is found in preaching the whole counsel of the Word of God under the anointing of the Spirit of God for the honor and glory of God alone. As Zechariah said, "Then he said to me, 'This is the word of the LORD to Zerubbabel: Not by might, nor by power, but by my Spirit, says the LORD of hosts" (Zech. 4:6).

About the Authors

Gary Wilkerson has served more than forty years in ministry. He is the president of World Challenge, an international mission organization that was founded by his father, David Wilkerson. Gary is also the founding pastor of The Springs Church, which he launched in 2009 with a handful of people. Gary frequently travels nationally and internationally to speak at conferences and to conduct mission ventures, such as planting churches and starting orphanages, clinics, and feeding programs among the poorest of the poor and the most unreached people of the earth.

Gary has written three books and hosts a podcast to address the tough questions that trip up many believers. Gary and his wife, Kelly, have four children and ten grandchildren. They live in Colorado Springs, Colorado.

Voddie T. Baucham, Jr. is a pastor, church planter, author of eight books, and professor known for his ability to demonstrate the Bible's relevance to everyday life without compromising the centrality of Christ and the gospel. He loves helping ordinary people understand the significance of thinking and living biblically in every area of life.

Currently, Voddie is the dean of the School of Divinity at African Christian University in Lusaka, Zambia. He and his wife, Bridget, have been married since 1989. They have nine children and three grandchildren. The Bauchams are committed home educators.

Carter Conlon serves as the general overseer of Times Square Church in New York City. He joined the pastoral staff as associate pastor in 1994 and was senior pastor from 2001 to 2020.

Carter has always demonstrated a passion for prayer, which is evidenced by his gathering of fifty thousand believers from many denominations to pray in the middle of Times Square. This led to two new ministries at Times Square Church—Feed New York, a ministry that supplies food assistance through local churches, and Worldwide Prayer Meeting, a weekly online prayer meeting that draws participants from 207 countries.

Carter hosts two syndicated radio shows, *It's Time to Pray* and *A Call to the Nation.* He has authored nine books, five of which are geared to children. He has preached around the globe. He continues to be a sought-after conference speaker.

Carter is married to Teresa, who is the president of Summit International School of Ministry and an associate pastor at Times Square Church. The Conlons have three children and eight grandchildren.

Tim Dilena has almost forty years of pastoral leadership and is currently the senior pastor of Times Square Church. Prior to the senior pastorate, he had been a frequent speaker at Times Square Church for over twenty-five years.

After pastoring a congregation in inner city Detroit for nearly thirty years, Tim joined The Brooklyn Tabernacle as associate pastor. After five years in Brooklyn, he joined Our Savior's Church in Lafayette, Louisiana, before returning to New York City in May 2020 to serve as senior pastor of Times Square Church.

Tim has been a regular speaker for the Major League Baseball and National Football League chapels. He is the author of *The 260 Journey,* a daily reading and devotional through the New Testament. Tim travels extensively with Gary Wilkerson and Nicky Cruz, speaking at global pastors conferences for World Challenge, where he also serves on the board of directors.

Tim and his wife, Cindy, have four children.

Claude Houde is the founder and senior pastor of New Life Church, one of the largest churches in Canada and the francophone world. An international speaker, Claude has brought a message of hope to more than fifty countries. He has authored four books and is the host of the *Café Matinal* podcast and YouTube channel.

Claude is president of the board of directors of the Christian Association for the Francophone World and chairman of the Institute of Theology for the Francophonie. He is a also a member of the board of directors of World Challenge.

Claude lives on the South Shore of Montreal with his wife Chantal and their children and grandchildren.

R. T. Kendall is a long-time writer, having authored over sixty books. He is also an international speaker and pastor. Born in Ashland, Kentucky, R. T. was educated at Southern Baptist Theological Seminary and Oxford University, where he began to pastor churches in the area. In 1977, he was invited to be the senior minister of London's Westminster Chapel, where he served for twenty-five years. R. T.'s deep desire is to see the church embrace both the Word and the Spirit through the sound doctrine of the Bible and the power and guidance of the Holy Spirit.

Now retired, R. T. and his wife, Louise, have two children and two grandchildren. They live in Cross Plains, Tennessee. He still writes and travels frequently to speak at conferences.

John Bailey is the vice president of ministry and operations at World Challenge, Inc. and the founding pastor of The Springs Church in Jacksonville, Florida. He came to know Christ in 1981 in the Tampa City Jail. John has now been serving the Lord in pastoral ministry for thirty-five years. He is a graduate of Southeastern University with a focus on pastoral ministry, systematic theology, and Bible. Since graduating, God has led him to minister the gospel in over fifty nations, particularly as a pastor, missionary, and evangelist to Cork, Ireland.

Joshua West is an author, evangelist, and pastor. He is currently the executive director of the pastors' and leaders' network at World Challenge, and he is also the director of World Challenge Publishing. Joshua comes from a background of life-controlling addiction. While in jail, the saving power of Christ radically transformed him. He has preached all over the world and has authored several books, including *Hard Sayings: Reconciling the Cost of Discipleship and the American Dream* and *Come and Die: Dying to Self and Living for Christ.*

The burning passion of Joshua's life is to boldly preach the gospel to a lost and dying world. He encourages believers to be conformed to the image of Christ through sound biblical preaching and teaching. He also has a great burden to equip and encourage pastors.

Joshua lives in Colorado Springs, Colorado, where he partners in life and ministry with his wife, Kiara. They have one son, Jameson.

About World Challenge

World Challenge, Inc. was founded in 1971 by Rev. David Wilkerson. It served as a corporate umbrella for Wilkerson's global ministries. Today, World Challenge has numerous mission outreaches to the poor, including orphanages, an overseas widows' fund, emergency/disaster relief, healthcare and clinics, community development, and feeding centers.

Gary Wilkerson became president of World Challenge in 2010 and moves forward with the same heart and vision as his father. Sermons from the Wilkersons are shared monthly through the *Pulpit Series* newsletter to hundreds of thousands of people.

This book is published in association with World Challenge.

Transforming lives through the message and mission of Jesus Christ.

For more information about
WORLD CHALLENGE
and
The Power of Preaching
please visit:

www.worldchallenge.org

World ⅄
Challenge
PUBLISHING

Ambassador International's mission is to magnify the Lord Jesus Christ and promote His Gospel through the written word.

We believe through the publication of Christian literature, Jesus Christ and His Word will be exalted, believers will be strengthened in their walk with Him, and the lost will be directed to Jesus Christ as the only way of salvation.

For more information about
AMBASSADOR INTERNATIONAL
please visit:

www.ambassador-international.com
@AmbassadorIntl
www.facebook.com/AmbassadorIntl

AMBASSADOR INTERNATIONAL
GREENVILLE, SOUTH CAROLINA & BELFAST, NORTHERN IRELAND

www.ambassador-international.com
Magnifying Jesus while promoting His gospel through the written word.

Thank you for reading this book!

You make it possible for us to fulfill our mission, and we are grateful for your partnership.

To help further our mission, please consider leaving us a review on your social media, favorite retailer's website, Goodreads or Bookbub, or our website, and check out some of our other books!

More from Ambassador International

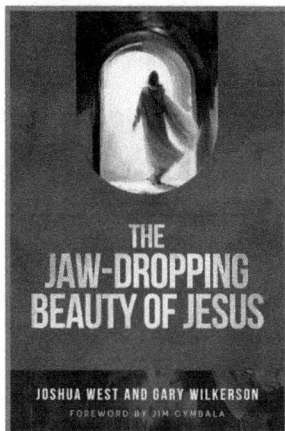

Most of us know Who Jesus is and would admit He was a good and kind Teacher while here on earth. But He is so much more than just a good and kind Teacher—He is our Savior and God and worthy of all our worship. Through an in-depth study into the book of Hebrews, Joshua West and Gary Wilkerson take apart each verse, drawing the reader to a closer look at the Man Who lived here on earth for a short time and then became our Sacrifice to save us from our sins and live with us eternally in Heaven with Him. If you are searching for something more from God, dive into this study and drink in the jaw-dropping beauty of our Jesus.

When our passions overtake us—as they often will—compulsive and addictive behaviors can set in. In *Misguided Passions and the Lord's Prayer*, Curt Richards examines the Lord's Prayer line by line and draws out comforting and reassuring insights that can be applied to the daily lives of anyone, especially those struggling with misguided passions. Richards shines a light on the beautiful universal truths found in the Lord's Prayer.

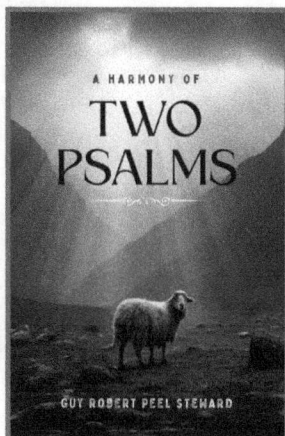

In a world that is full of chaos and change, many people turn to the Psalms to find comfort in times of stress. In *A Harmony of Two Psalms*, Guy Robert Peel Steward takes a closer look at two of those psalms—Psalm 2 and 91—and analyzes their key truths, hoping to shine some light for the reader on what the words truly mean and how they can find comfort in the God Who sees the chaos and offers rest in the storm. Be challenged in your knowledge of God's Word and learn more about some of the verses that can soothe our weary souls.